SUFFOLK

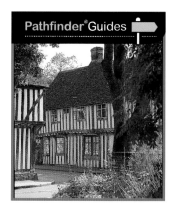

Pathfinder®Guides

Outstanding
Circular Walks

Compiled by John Brooks
Revised by Deborah King

Contents

At-a-glance	2	Slightly harder walks of 3 - 3½ hours	48
Keymap and Introduction	4	Longer walks of 4 hours and over	75
Short walks up to 2½ hours	9	Further Information	92

At-a-glance

Walk		Page	🧭	🏢	🚩	⛰	🕐
1	Carlton Marshes and the River Waveney	10	Carlton Marshes Visitor Centre	TM 508 920	2¾ miles (4.4km)	N/a	1½ hrs
2	Southwold	12	Southwold pier	TM 511 767	3¾ miles (6km)	N/a	1½ hrs
3	Darmsden and the Gipping Valley	14	Needham Lake, Needham Market	TM 093 546	4¼ miles (6.8km)	180ft (55m)	2 hrs
4	Nowton Park and High Suffolk	16	Nowton Park	TL 864 621	4½ miles (7.2km)	180ft (55m)	2 hrs
5	Stoke-by-Nayland to Polstead	18	Stoke-by-Nayland church	TL 986 362	4½ miles (7km)	330ft (100m)	2 hrs
6	Shingle Street and Alderton	20	Shingle Street	TM 369 431	4½ miles (7.2km)	N/a	2 hrs
7	Pakenham Mills from Ixworth	22	Ixworth	TL 932 703	5 miles (8km)	100ft (30m)	2½ hrs
8	Covehithe and Benacre	24	Covehithe	TM 521 818	5½ miles (8.9km)	100ft (30m)	2½ hrs
9	Cretingham and Brandeston	26	Cretingham	TM 227 603	5 miles (8km)	215ft (65m)	2½ hrs
10	Forest and riverside from West Stow	28	Forest Lodge, West Stow	TL 815 714	5¼ miles (8.4km)	115ft (35m)	2½ hrs
11	Eye and Braiseworth	30	Buckshorn Lane, Eye	TM 145 738	5 miles (8km)	150ft (45m)	2½ hrs
12	Framlingham and its countryside	33	Framlingham	TM 282 635	5½ miles (8.8km)	165ft (50m)	2½ hrs
13	Constable Country – Flatford and East Bergholt	36	East Bergholt	TM 069 346	5½ miles (8.9km)	230ft (70m)	2½ hrs
14	Long Melford	39	Long Melford	TL 865 466	5½ miles (8.8km)	230ft (70m)	2½ hrs
15	Somerleyton and Waddling Lane	43	Somerleyton	TM 478 971	6¼ miles (10.1km)	N/a	2½ hrs
16	West Row and Worlington from Mildenhall	46	Mildenhall	TL 712 744	6¼ miles (10.1km)	N/a	2½ hrs
17	Orford coast and country	49	Orford	TM 424 496	6¼ miles (10.1km)	100ft (30m)	3 hrs
18	Thorpeness from Leiston	52	Leiston Leisure Centre	TM 451 619	6½ miles (10.5km)	N/a	3 hrs
19	Saxmundham, Kelsale and the Gull Stream	55	Saxmundham	TM 386 632	7 miles (11.3km)	215ft (65m)	3 hrs
20	Lavenham and Brent Eleigh	58	Lavenham	TL 914 489	7¼ miles (11.6km)	230ft (70m)	3½ hrs
21	Sudbury and its water meadows	61	Rodbridge	TL 857 437	7½ miles (12km)	150ft (45m)	3½ hrs
22	Clare and Cavendish	64	Clare Country Park	TL 770 451	7½ miles (11.9km)	310ft (95m)	3½ hrs
23	Iken and Tunstall Forest	68	Snape Maltings	TM 393 573	7¾ miles (12.3km)	150ft (45m)	3½ hrs
24	Barham, Baylham and Coddenham	71	Gipping Valley Centre	TM 123 512	8 miles (12.9km)	230ft (70m)	3½ hrs
25	Kersey and Hadleigh	76	The ford, Kersey	TM 000 441	8¼ miles (13.2km)	410ft (125m)	4 hrs
26	Thorpe Morieux to Preston St Mary	80	Bury Road, Thorpe Morieux	TL 942 538	9 miles (14.4km)	475ft (145m)	4 hrs
27	Denham Castle and the three churches	84	Packhorse Bridge, Moulton	TL 697 645	9¼ miles (14.9km)	395ft (120m)	4 hrs
28	Sutton Hoo, Shottisham and the River Deben	88	Sutton Heath	TM 306 475	10 miles (16.1km)	295ft (90m)	4½ hrs

Comments

This walk through marshland south of Lowestoft reaches an isolated section of the bank of the River Waveney. The return passes Sprat's Water – a wonderful habitat for reedbed birds.

There are many good reasons to visit Southwold, among them its interesting buildings, including the huts on the promenade. Fresh fish can be bought from the huts by the river, also passed en route.

Climb to the windswept countryside above Needham Market and then descend to the sheltered bank of the River Gipping, a delightful waterway that is the haunt of herons, kingfishers and otters.

This is a delightful walk through the mature parkland of Nowton Park on the edge of Bury St Edmunds. An interesting stretch of footpath is a prelude to a return through the park.

A walk through historic villages with fine views of countryside that is surprisingly hilly for East Anglia. It includes three pubs and two churches, one of which appears in several paintings by Constable.

One can easily imagine smugglers and wreckers of bygone days on the beach at Shingle Street. The walk uses the flood wall and field paths to take you to Alderton and its pub.

This short walk starts at Ixworth and is on bridleways and quiet lanes. It goes across lonely countryside and by two lovely mills, one powered by the wind, the other by water.

The coastline between Covehithe and Benacre suffers badly from erosion and tree stumps upright on the beach show how much has been lost. Benacre Broad is an RSPB reserve.

The beautiful landscape of the upper River Deben is well seen in this circuit beginning in the pleasant village of Cretingham. There is an excellent selection of footpaths serving this neighbourhood.

Forest, sandy field tracks, timbered parkland and quiet riverside are combined to illustrate the varied landscapes of Breckland in north west Suffolk.

Eye is a country town isolated from main roads. The church and castle and other fine buildings reflect its former importance and the walk shows the best of the surrounding countryside.

Highlights include the tombs and effigies in St Michael's Church in Framlingham and footpaths around the town that offer superb views of the castle and its Mere, now part of a wildlife reserve.

Connoisseurs of the English landscape flock to Dedham Vale to try to recognise features that Constable painted. This walk passes one of his most famous viewpoints as well as Flatford Mill itself.

A walk that passes the imposing church of Long Melford before entering the grounds to Kentwell Hall, a historical great house. Many of the paths are through meadows and arable fields.

Somerleyton is one of the most attractive Broadland villages, its pretty cottages matching the architecture of Somerleyton Hall. The walk is on tracks and paths around the outskirts of the estate.

Suffolk's western boundary lies in fenland, which is sometimes unfairly dismissed as being uninteresting. Those who tackle this route will find the River Lark delightful and the horizons immense.

Orford was a busy seaport until the 17th century, when its river began to be choked by silt. The castle is often in view during the walk. Dating from 1165 it is polygonal – a revolutionary design at the time.

This walk is a good mix of seaside and countryside – the former following the coast path from Sizewell to Thorpeness while the latter is mainly on field paths over heath and arable land.

The walk follows an attractive stream to the lakes at its source. Some of the paths cross fields that may have crops and are often muddy in winter.

Timber-framed houses, historic wall paintings and a nature reserve are to be found on this pleasant walk from Lavenham to tiny Brent Eleigh and its 13th century church.

Ancient water meadows, two mills and a disused railway line provide tranquility on this lovely walk that passes through the market town of Sudbury.

A pleasant walk starting from the village of Clare where the motte of a Norman Castle can be seen. The route follows the Stour Valley Path to Cavendish and crosses the River Stour twice.

This will be a favourite walk with many people as it combines a lovely estuary section with a return through equally attractive forest. This is an excellent all season route.

A delightful beginning by lakes and riverside before the way crosses the busy A14 and climbs through woodland to beautiful Coddenham. The way back is through parkland surrounding Shrubland Hall.

None of Suffolk's 'chocolate box' villages is more famous or picturesque than Kersey. The walk is a satisfying ramble covering a wide tract of farmland. Spare time to see Hadleigh's medieval buildings.

This walk shows rural Suffolk at its best with a mixture of quiet country lanes, field edge paths and bridleways. The return leg passes a good pub.

The 'Three Churches Walk' has long been famous and is a fine way of sampling the scenery in the west of the county. Although nothing remains of Denham Castle this part provides magnificent views.

Birdwatchers and archaeologists will particularly enjoy the landscape of heath and estuary covered on this route. The path along the low cliff above the Deben is underused and may be overgrown.

Introduction to Suffolk

Suffolk is a reticent county. Its landscapes are never spectacular and may, in a few places in the midst of its prairie-like corn belt, lack character. Yet the riverside meadows of the Stour Valley are the ones that Constable painted and they remain as beautiful today as when he portrayed them two centuries ago. In the same way, and a highest point just 128m (420ft) above sea level. Oak forest veiled much of its countryside until the 18th century, but most of this fell to axe and saw when the navy had to enlarge its fleet against the threat posed by Napoleon.

More or less coincidentally with the felling of the forest, Acts of Inclosure enabled landowners to enlarge their

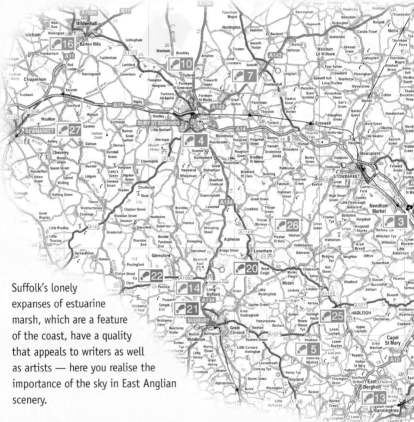

Suffolk's lonely expanses of estuarine marsh, which are a feature of the coast, have a quality that appeals to writers as well as artists — here you realise the importance of the sky in East Anglian scenery.

The evolution of the countryside

Suffolk is the easternmost county of England with an area of 1,466 sq miles (3,797 sq km), a population of 714,000, estates by taking over common lands. These had supplied free grazing and firewood for generations of villagers so when the privileges were withdrawn many of them were left destitute. Some emigrated to America and Australia while others took work in the emerging industrial towns.

The agricultural depression of the 1930s saw many more people forced from their land. This time it affected farmers who had long struggled to make a living from a few acres of small fields

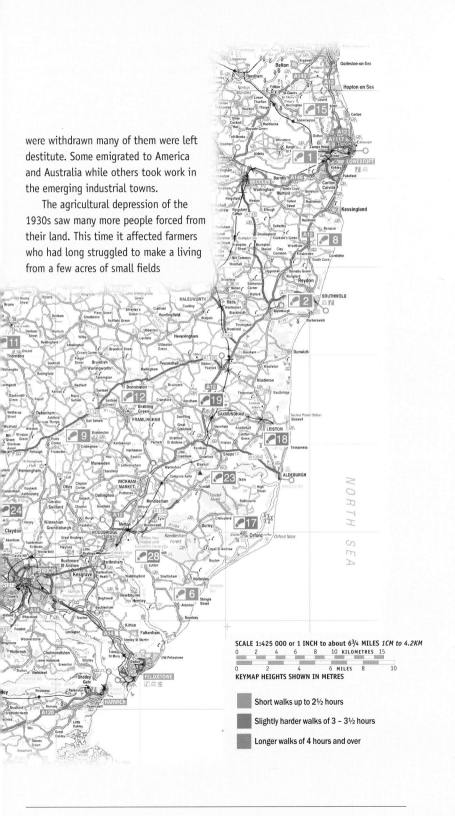

SCALE 1:425 000 or 1 INCH to about 6¾ MILES *1CM to 4.2KM*

0   2   4   6   8   10 KILOMETRES 15

0   2   4   6 MILES   8   10

KEYMAP HEIGHTS SHOWN IN METRES

Short walks up to 2½ hours

Slightly harder walks of 3 – 3½ hours

Longer walks of 4 hours and over

bounded by sturdy hedges. Many of their farms were bought by neighbouring, wealthier landowners but Scottish farmers also took advantage of the low prices. Fields were merged to make units more suitable for cultivation by tractors and so began a process that has continued into the 21st century. Fortunately, we are beginning to recognise the damage to wildlife caused by removing ditches, ponds and hedges but there are many places in the county where above endless acres of grain or sugar beet the skylark no longer sings.

The buildings of Suffolk

The geology of the county is simple, with a dome of chalk having been covered by layers of different clays when the glaciers retreated at the end of the Ice Age. The clays suited deciduous woodland that provided the main landscape feature of inland Suffolk until the 18th century. These three ingredients provided the basic building materials that give Suffolk's ancient buildings their character.

Flints were mined from chalk and 'knapped' to produce dark hued building stone of uniform size. This is to be seen in the grander churches of the county, often worked into decorative panels with imported stone. More humble churches, and domestic and farm buildings, were often made of unworked flints picked from the fields or beach.

The various Suffolk clays were used for brickmaking from the 15th century, reviving a craft lost since Roman times. The county is particularly well endowed with brick-built mansions, and much brickwork is also to be seen in churches as well as in the castles at Orford and Framlingham.

The enduring quality of oak timber as a building material is seen all over Suffolk in exterior and interior work. Some of the most intricate examples of hammerbeam roofs are in Suffolk churches, those at Mildenhall and Needham Market being outstanding 'wooden visions of paradise'. The genius of Suffolk carpenters from different eras is also shown brilliantly at Dennington, where you may see a medieval carving of the Sciapod, a bizarre humanoid whose feet are as long as his body, with a Jacobean three decker pulpit and a fine set of box pews of 1725.

Suffolk has 500 medieval churches, and each has some important architectural or historical feature. The magnificence of churches such as those at Long Melford or Lavenham derives from local entrepreneurs who became wealthy by raising sheep or weaving the wool they produced. By endowing these wonderful churches the merchants hoped they would reap rewards in heaven. Certainly the generations that followed them have been grateful for the splendour created by the masons and carpenters.

Timber was also a vital ingredient in domestic architecture, as a visit to Lavenham or any other famously pretty village will show. Because of the considerable labour that was required to transform tree trunks into beams with relatively smooth edges, parts of the timber frame will probably have served other buildings before being used in the one where you see it today. The tree that it came from may have been felled 600 years ago. It is this sort of improvisation that makes the old houses of Suffolk so picturesque.

Writers, painters and a composer

The poetry of George Crabbe reflects the dire poverty suffered in rural Suffolk 200 or so years ago as well as the beauty of the landscape of east Suffolk. His verse beach of Shingle Street in the gloomy dusk of a November day it is easy to imagine being waylaid by the ghost of a smuggler. Anyone interested in the life of ordinary people in Suffolk in the 19th and early 20th centuries is recommended to read Ronald Blythe's *Akenfield*, a work written in the 1960s that has become a classic.

Reedbeds are a common feature of the Suffolk landscape

appealed to another Suffolk genius, Benjamin Britten, who set Crabbe's words to music in his opera *Peter Grimes*. The lonely salt marshes around Aldeburgh also inspired orchestral music such as the evocative *Sea Interludes*. The world famous concert hall that overlooks the marshes at Snape Maltings celebrates Benjamin Britten and is the venue for an outstanding annual music festival. The complex also provides facilities to encourage promising young musicians to develop their talents.

M.R. James used the same district as a setting for some of his ghost stories, and while walking along the deserted

Of the many artists who have found inspiration in the Suffolk landscape two are immortal. John Constable was born at East Bergholt in 1776 and intended to be a portrait painter. However, he loved to paint landscapes and found inspiration for them in the everyday scenes that he saw in the Stour Valley. He was 35 years old when his landscape of Dedham Vale made him known, and this was followed by further masterpieces such as *The Leaping Horse* and *The Hay Wain*. His work was never as popular in England as in France until after his death in 1827. Thomas Gainsborough was born in 1727 in Sudbury and trained in London before returning to Suffolk. Although most famous for his portraits of the rich and famous, Gainsborough's real passion was for landscapes and this must have derived from his upbringing in Suffolk.

Practical walking

With some 9,800 registered rights of way and a path network of more than 3,500 miles (5,600km), Suffolk offers plenty of scope for countryside walking. Numerous long distance walks weave through the county and there is endless opportunity for shorter circular walks focusing on the places of interest and beauty spots that abound. Part of the Broads National Park lies within the boundaries of the county as well as two Areas of Outstanding Natural Beauty; Dedham Vale and Suffolk Coast and Heaths. Recent legislation has created many Access Areas, which includes extensive stretches of forest and heath. Such variety offers a wealth of different landscapes to explore.

The gentle, rolling terrain with few strenuous hills lends itself to undemanding walking, but this in no way diminishes the satisfaction to be gained from a day's ramble. While the warnings that apply to upland or wilderness areas are here less relevant, a few simple, common-sense precautions will contribute to the comfort and pleasure of a day out. Rutted tracks, hidden rabbit holes, wet ground and tree roots are ever-present hazards and comfortable, waterproof boots that give support to the ankles are infinitely preferable to trainers or light shoes. As anywhere else in the country, the weather can be unpredictable and coastal winds may be unexpectedly cold, so it is always a good idea to carry waterproofs and something warm. During summer, suncream and a hat will guard against burning and a good supply of water or soft drink will help avoid the ill-effects of dehydration. On a fine day, the thought of shorts and T-shirts is often inviting, but more sensible are trousers and a sleeved shirt to protect against the nettles and brambles inevitably encountered during the summer months. While many of the routes pass a refreshment stop during the course of the day, it is always a good idea to carry a snack to sustain you should your plans change or the pub be shut.

Suffolk's footpath officers and rangers work hard to keep the path network passable, but if you encounter an obstruction, damaged stile or gate, you will help their task by reporting it. There are contact numbers in the 'Further Information' section of this guide: the Broads Authority for within the National Park or the County Council elsewhere. Give a date and clear description of the problem with an accurate location, including a map reference if possible.

This book includes a list of waypoints alongside the description of the walk, so that you can enjoy the full benefits of gps should you wish to. For more information on using your gps, read the Pathfinder® Guide *GPS for Walkers*, by gps teacher and navigation trainer, Clive Thomas (ISBN 978-0-7117-4445-5). For essential information on map reading and basic navigation, read the Pathfinder® Guide *Map Reading Skills* by outdoor writer, Terry Marsh (ISBN 978-0-7117-4978-8). Both titles are available in bookshops or can be ordered online at www.pathfinderwalks.co.uk

St Mary's Church,
Stoke by Nayland

walk 1

✎ Start
Carlton Marshes Visitor Centre, Burnt Hill Lane, Carlton Colville

⌁ Distance
2¾ miles (4.4km)

Ⱉ Height gain
Negligible

◷ Approximate time
1½ hours

⬧ Route terrain
Recreational paths and footpaths beside marsh

Ⓟ Parking
Car park at start

⌖ OS maps
Landranger 134 (Norwich & The Broads), Explorer OL40 (The Broads)

▣ GPS waypoints
✎ TM 508 920
Ⓐ TM 500 926
Ⓑ TM 494 930
Ⓒ TM 493 927
Ⓓ TM 503 916

Carlton Marshes and the River Waveney

The Suffolk Wildlife Trust owns 100 acres (40ha) of grazing marshes, fen and peat pools within an area bounded by the River Waveney to the north and the railway to the south. It is an invaluable reserve reflecting all the different Broadland habitats within a compact area. The paths followed on the walk are all rights of way, though there is an interesting diversion to Sprat's Water towards the end of the walk for those without dogs.

The marshes are full of interest at any time of year but in winter it is a place to wrap up warmly - otherwise you will be in no doubt that Suffolk's east wind blows directly from the Urals. At the visitor centre you can find out about the rare varieties of plants, insects and birds that you may encounter here.

✎ Turn right along the main track, passing through a gate onto the reserve. Over to the right are White Cast Marshes, where the Waveney flows into Oulton Broad. The reed beds are rigorously protected during the breeding season when marsh harriers nest. You might also hear the booming cry of the male bittern from the watery wilderness, a welcome sound heralding the comeback of this secretive bird. In 1997 there were only 11 breeding males left in the country, but extension and management of the reed beds has increased numbers to 30, some of which are found in Norfolk and Suffolk.

In time the main track swings right towards Oulton Dyke Ⓐ. Leave there, continuing ahead through a gate towards a cattle pen. Parting company with the grass track beyond it, walk to a stile in the far-right corner. Keep going with the ditch now on your left.

Peto's Marsh, to the right, takes its name from the Victorian railway magnate who rebuilt Somerleyton Hall. The vast expanse of cultivated land and grazing reflects the efficiency of the steam, diesel and electric pumps that in turn replaced the windmills, which first pumped water from dyke to river.

Steps lead up to the riverbank Ⓑ, now well above the surrounding marshes, which have progressively sunk as a result of the drainage. Turn left beside the Waveney, which in summer is busy with pleasure craft but utterly deserted during the winter months, shortly reaching a hardstanding, the site of the Share Drainage Mill. A hunk of metalwork is all that remains of the old water pump, its modern counterpart concealed within

Share Marsh, Carlton Colville

a low concrete bunker. Leave the embankment just beyond, dropping to a bridge **C**.

Follow a grass track across the marshes for a mile, eventually winding to a junction **D**. The path opposite enters the conservation area around Sprat's Water, rejoining the main route a little farther on. *However, those with*

dogs must turn left. Carry on past a bridge, over which the reserve path emerges, and through a couple of gates to a fork. The surfaced path to the right winds beside a final length of ditch, returning you to the start point. ●

0	200	400	600	800 METRES	1

KILOMETRES
MILES

0	200	400	600 YARDS	½

SCALE 1:25 000 or 2½ INCHES to 1 MILE 4CM to 1KM

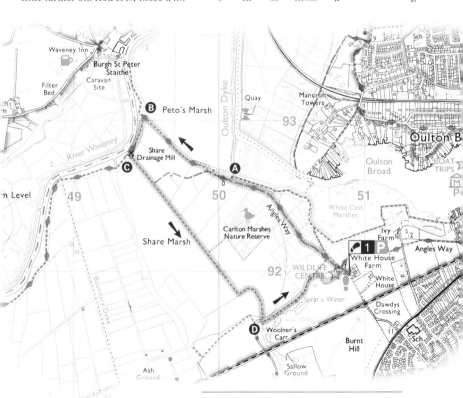

Southwold

Start

Southwold pier

Distance

3¾ miles (6km)

Height gain

Negligible

Approximate time

1½ hours

Route terrain

Grassy paths beside marshes, coastal paths

P Parking

Car park to north of pier

OS maps

Landranger 156 (Saxmundham), Explorer 231 (Southwold & Bungay)

GPS waypoints

TM 511 767
Ⓐ TM 512 769
Ⓑ TM 504 768
Ⓒ TM 494 758
Ⓓ TM 501 750

Southwold's character stems chiefly from the diverse architecture of its seafront. This walk around its island shows that it has far more to offer – a river busy with fishing and pleasure craft and lonely marshes beautiful beneath a wide East Anglian sky.

Walk northwards from the pier past a row of colourful beach huts beside the car park. Turn left just before the top end of the car park Ⓐ onto a footpath that heads past the boating lake and across the marshes.

To the left the lake is a haven for waterfowl, especially in winter when visiting geese dispute territory with resident species. Behind, the town presents a fine picture with the light-house and church breaking the skyline, a different aspect to that normally seen from the greens or seafront.

Cross the road beside Might's Bridge Ⓑ and take the footpath on the south side of Buss Creek to continue around the circumference of the island. The creek is a popular venue with anglers, and its meandering course provides pleasant walking. Keep ahead past a kissing-gate as another footpath crosses, the way developing a wonderful air of remoteness as apparent signs of habitation become more distant. Go through a gate and then farther on the banktop path swings around, giving another view of Southwold in which the water tower, so deplored by the art historian Pevsner, is prominent.

Within a short distance the path turns southwards, passing the debouchement of the creek where it falls into the River Blyth. Just beyond, the piers that once carried the railway line

Southwold beach

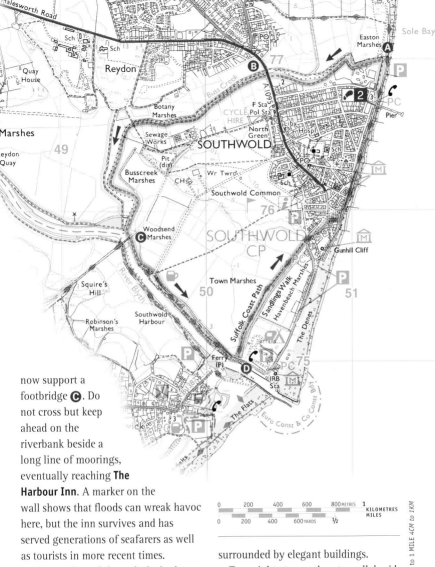

now support a footbridge **C**. Do not cross but keep ahead on the riverbank beside a long line of moorings, eventually reaching **The Harbour Inn**. A marker on the wall shows that floods can wreak havoc here, but the inn survives and has served generations of seafarers as well as tourists in more recent times.

The rough road through the harbour continues past boatyards, chandlers, fish shops and idiosyncratic fishermen's huts. When all these end, turn left just after the last telegraph pole before a caravan site onto a path beneath a flood bank **D**. This passes through thorn thicket and then runs on at the edge of the marsh, giving a fine prospect of the town in which the church, lighthouse and Adnams brewery can all be seen. Keep ahead when this meets a road at the edge of South Green, a delightful open space

surrounded by elegant buildings.

Turn right at a postbox to walk beside Acton Lodge to the seafront and go left along the promenade to return to the pier. Southwold is one of the country's most attractive seaside resorts, with a row of splendid buildings overlooking the sea that date mainly from Regency and early Victorian times when the town became fashionable. Beyond St James Green are the lighthouse, **Sole Bay Inn** and the brewery, but the line of old hotels is broken as several were destroyed during the Second World War.

SCALE 1:25 000 or 2½ INCHES to 1 MILE 4CM to 1KM

walk 3

Start
Needham Lake,
Needham Market

Distance
4¼ miles (6.8km)

Height gain
180 feet (55m)

Approximate time
2 hours

Route terrain
Towpath, gravel tracks,
some road walking

Parking
Car park at start

OS maps
Landranger 155 (Bury
St Edmunds), Explorer
211 (Bury St Edmunds
& Stowmarket)

GPS waypoints
📷 TM 093 546
Ⓐ TM 091 549
Ⓑ TM 091 543
Ⓒ TM 090 533
Ⓓ TM 100 533
Ⓔ TM 107 536

Darmsden and the Gipping Valley

The towpath between Stowmarket and Ipswich following the River Gipping, a commercial waterway in the 19th century, makes an excellent linear walk. This circular route takes in scenery of higher ground and a lovely hamlet overlooking the valley as well as the beautiful towpath.

📷 There are two car parks at Needham Lake and if you park in the one on the eastern side you will have to cross the footbridge to reach the one nearest the main road, where there are public toilets. Walk beside the lake past the rangers' office, continuing below the railway embankment at the edge of open meadow. Reaching a waypost Ⓐ, turn left and duck your head to pass through a low tunnel beneath the railway, emerging beside the Victorian station. Keep ahead through Station Yard to the High Street opposite **The Swan Inn**. Go left along Ipswich Road, leaving right up Grinsted Hill when you reach **The Lion Inn**. After 100 yds turn left onto a footpath at a public footpath signpost Ⓑ.

The path is enclosed as it climbs past chalk quarries on the left. Carry on at the top of the hill as it emerges into fields, where Darmsden chapel is an obvious landmark ahead. Bear right when the track divides, staying with it as it bends right to reach a junction of paths. Turn left and, when you reach a gravel track, go left again Ⓒ, rising beyond a dip to the chapel. It is a lovely little building and still in use even though there is no electricity. It dates from 1888 and served about 70 souls when it was built, but just a handful attend today.

Keep ahead as you join a lane just beyond the chapel, shortly bearing left at a junction to walk past cottages and Darmsden Hall. There is then a view right to Shrubland Hall, a spectacular Italianate mansion remodelled by Sir Charles Barry between 1848 and 1852. Entering Chalkpit Plantation, look for a waymarked path on the right Ⓓ that descends through the trees. Continue at the edge of the wood and then across a field to meet the main road by a rusting tin hut. Turn right for 100 yds before going left over a stile beside a gate at the entrance to a landfill site. Where the track bends left, keep ahead to cross the railway line and carry on over open ground to reach the River Gipping at Pipps Ford Lock Ⓔ.

Turn left along the bank, an excellent habitat for a wide variety of birdlife. In winter the bordering meadows are often flooded but it is unusual to find the path impassable. Footbridges take the route across a loop of the river created to serve a watermill that has long since gone. There is another former lock at Riverside Farm, beyond which is a particularly pretty stretch that runs beneath poplars. Passing a fishing lake, a grass track develops that leads to the road by a converted watermill. Turning right, cross both the

Swans on the River Gipping

road and the river, dropping into a field beside it. Walk up past the mill and Bosmere Lock to the eastern car park, re-crossing the river back to the start. ●

SCALE 1:25000 or 2½ INCHES to 1 MILE 4CM to 1KM

Start

Nowton Park, Bury St
Edmunds (to south of
town)

Distance

4½ miles (7.2km)

Height gain

180 feet (55m)

Approximate time

2 hours

Route terrain

Grass, woodland and
bridleways

P Parking

Car park at start

OS maps

Landranger 155 (Bury
St Edmunds), Explorer
211 (Bury St Edmunds
& Stowmarket)

GPS waypoints

- TL 864 621
- Ⓐ TL 861 622
- Ⓑ TL 860 615
- Ⓒ TL 851 613
- Ⓓ TL 858 605
- Ⓔ TL 865 607
- Ⓕ TL 865 612

Nowton Park and High Suffolk

*This delightful ramble follows the Bury to Clare Walk on to High
Suffolk, a tract of elevated land south of Bury St Edmunds.
After visiting an isolated church, the way returns through the
200-acre (81 ha) Nowton Park.*

Before its acquisition by Bury Corporation in 1985, Nowton
Court and park belonged to the Oakes family. A banker and
County Treasurer, Oakes built a 'large and handsome mansion'
and planted the famous Lime Avenue as well as an arboretum
containing both native species and specimen trees from around
the world.

 Walk to the end of the car park farthest from the Ranger
Centre and toilets, where there is a noticeboard marking the
start of the Bury to Clare Walk, a meandering route of around
18½ miles amongst some of the finest scenery of 'High Suffolk'.
Follow the path through trees to the road and go right. Opposite
Plovers' Way, abandon it for a bridleway on the left. Carry on
past the entrance to Breckley Ley house, swinging left where
the way splits at the corner of the grounds Ⓐ. Remain beside
the wood at the edge of open country, meeting a lane at the
end. Follow it ahead for some 550 yds before leaving right Ⓑ
onto an inviting grassy bridleway that rises gently between the
fields. Near the summit of the hill is a crossing of paths Ⓒ. Go
left and, in the field corner by a stand of trees, cross a ditch to
continue on its opposite flank past a triangulation pillar,
eventually meeting Park Lane.

Now parting company with the Bury to Clare Walk, follow
the lane left, a quiet, broad-verged byway that allows views
over a wide tract of countryside. To the left is Bury and the
chimney of a large sugar beet factory, a long plume of white
smoke often emanating from its chimney. When the lane bends
sharply left by a thatched cottage, keep ahead on a gravel track.
After 20 yds, leave over a stile on the left Ⓓ and strike a
diagonal across a meadow, where decaying oak trees show it
once to have been parkland belonging to Nowton Hall. Climb a
stile in the far corner to walk through a paddock behind a barn.
Cross a farm drive and then another meadow before reaching
St Peter's Church, hidden behind trees until the last moment.
The small Norman church was founded for monks from
St Edmund's Abbey who worked in vineyards on these rolling

In Nowton Park

hills; the chancel was added early in the 14th century. After the Dissolution, the church remained in use by the villagers and was restored in 1843.

Follow the lane left to a road **E** and go left again into the hamlet. Keep left when the road later bends in front of a junction. Just after the pavement ends, look for a gate on the right into Nowton Park **F**. Disregarding the 'Private' sign, go through to a waymarked path. Several walks lead to the park's many features: an arboretum, a maze, wildflower meadows, ponds and a bird hide. One of the showpieces is Lime Avenue, which in spring is ablaze with countless daffodils. *The quickest way*

back is along the waymarked circular walk to the left, which ultimately returns you to the Ranger Centre along Lime Avenue. But to see more of the park, instead turn right past the totem pole, following yellow waymarkers and later entering woodland at a yellow and blue waymarked post. Eventually, approaching playing fields, you can bear left across the park or stay with the wooded perimeter, either way returning to the car park. ●

SCALE 1:25000 or 2½ INCHES to 1 MILE 4CM to 1KM

0	200	400	600	800 METRES	**1**
					KILOMETRES
					MILES
0	200	400	600 YARDS	½	

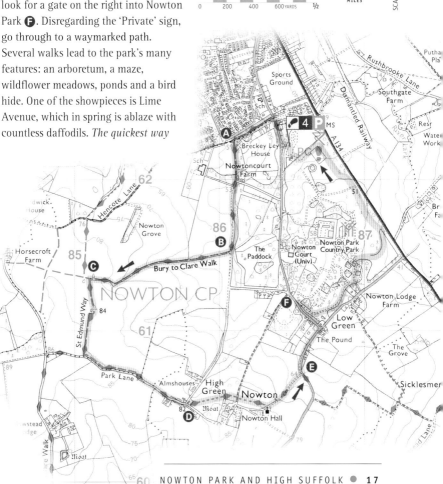

Start

Stoke-by-Nayland church

Distance

4½ miles (7km)

Height gain

330 feet (100m)

Approximate time

2 hours

Route terrain

Grassy paths, woodland, quiet lanes

Parking

Parking in Church Street

OS maps

Landranger 155 (Bury St Edmunds), Explorer 196 (Sudbury, Hadleigh & Dedham Vale)

GPS waypoints

TL 986 362
Ⓐ TL 993 366
Ⓑ TL 989 377
Ⓒ TL 992 378
Ⓓ TL 997 372
Ⓔ TL 997 363

Stoke-by–Nayland to Polstead

An enjoyable ramble that is surprisingly hilly by East Anglian standards. The route through water meadows and pastures links two pretty villages with historic interest and there are some outstanding views.

The tower of St Mary's Church in Stoke-by-Nayland dominates the landscape and appears in several of Constable's paintings. Inside this magnificent church there are some Tudor tombs with links to Catherine Howard, Henry VIII's fifth wife, who was later beheaded at the Tower of London.

Facing the porch of St Mary's Church, turn right and keep ahead to leave the churchyard, passing to the left of a small green and continuing left along Church Street. At the next junction by the **Angel Inn**, cross the road to Scotland Street and continue downhill past thatched cottages. Just after some white painted railings turn left at a public footpath sign Ⓐ. Walk through a thicket and emerge at a field edge then turn left and head gently uphill – to the right there is a view of Polstead church in the distance. At a field corner follow the way-marked path right which heads downhill and at the bottom walk on through a hedge gap to a well-used track and turn left. Keep ahead along the track, which soon becomes pasture for livestock, and later go over a stile to emerge onto a road.

Turn right here and continue along the quiet road, go over a bridge, which crosses the River Box, and at a right-hand bend walk ahead to a metal kissing-gate Ⓑ.

Enter a meadow and walk uphill towards Polstead church and its ancient oak tree and imposing war memorial, which is one of the biggest in the country. Enter the churchyard through a kissing-gate and head for the porch entrance. Turn right, following the path as it skirts the church, and leave the churchyard through a wooden gate. Head downhill towards an impressive village pond. Turn right at the road and continue gently downhill – the village centre can be visited by taking the first road to the left. Continue along the road and where the road bends right keep ahead to a stile Ⓒ.

Follow the field path as it heads up a steep hill to the summit from where there are fine views of both Stoke-by-Nayland and Polstead. Continue along the path where it levels out and at a field corner take the path to the left towards a metal kissing-gate. Keep ahead between paddock fencing and a hedge and at a lane turn right and take the footpath immediately to the left. Continue ahead between more paddocks until reaching a T-junction. Here, turn right along a farm track as it descends and where the track bears right towards farm buildings, keep ahead and follow the path as it curves right towards a wooden gate **D**.

Do not go through the gate but turn left to follow the waymarked path into woodland. Exit the wood following the grass track to the right and continue downhill until the path curves right to a metal kissing-gate. Go through this to enter a water meadow and follow the path to the left of a lake, leaving the meadow through a kissing-gate before crossing a footbridge to the road. Turn right and cross the River Box over a road bridge. Take the next footpath to the left and climb a stile, then continue along the

Village pond, Polstead

Stour Valley Path and go through a wooden kissing-gate on the right **E**.

The field path continues right and uphill to another wooden kissing-gate opposite. Go through a thicket and emerge at a metal kissing-gate to enter rolling farm land and continue uphill to the left of a hedge. The path curves left at the back of gardens and descends to a crossing of paths at a field corner. Take the path to the left and walk uphill to the left of a hedge to reach a metal kissing-gate at a road. Turn right and follow the path towards Stoke-by-Nayland village, past **The Crown** pub and then turn left into Church Street and retrace your steps to the start of the walk. ●

SCALE 1:25 000 or 2½ INCHES to 1 MILE 4CM to 1KM

Start

Coastguard cottages, Shingle Street

Distance

4½ miles (7.2km)

Height gain

Negligible

Approximate time

2 hours

Route terrain

Shingle beach, grazing pasture

Parking

Car park at start

Dog friendly

Keep on lead to point **B**

OS maps

Landranger 169 (Ipswich & The Naze), Explorer 197 (Ipswich, Felixstowe & Harwich)

GPS waypoints

- TM 369 431
- **A** TM 366 425
- **B** TM 363 424
- **C** TM 360 416
- **D** TM 356 416
- **E** TM 345 423

Shingle Street and Alderton

Shingle Street is just that, a lonely row of houses and cottages behind a beach of small stones, which in spring becomes a nesting site for ringed plovers and little terns. This short walk takes in the pleasant village of Alderton as well as two of the Martello towers built between 1810 and 1812 to guard the coast against French invasion.

Park before the coastguard cottages, walk past an information board to the beach and turn right to head south-wards along the shore.

The sea has graded the pebbles so that the smaller ones are nearer the sea. The shingle supports several rare plants right up to the tideline, including the sea pea (*Lathyrus japonicus*) and yellow horned poppy (*Glaucium flavum*). Little terns fly here from Africa in the spring to nest, so in this season it is best to walk below the tideline and keep dogs on the lead.

Beyond the cottages, leave the beach for a fenced path beside the Martello tower **A**. These copied the design of a coastal tower seen by Royal Engineers at Martella in Corsica in 1794, and were part of countrywide coastal defences against a threatened Napoleonic invasion. Most of those surviving have been converted into residences or holiday homes.

Bear left on a beaten path across the grazing marsh to a point on the flood bank where it is crossed by telephone lines **B**.

Martello towers built as defence against Napoleonic invasion

Second World War defences are to be seen on the marshes to the left in the form of pillboxes and concrete tank traps, whilst offshore container ships often lie waiting for high tide to take them into Felixstowe. Walk left along the bank, passing another Martello tower, this one deserted and topped by a wartime machine gun emplacement.

A third Martello tower lies ahead, but about halfway between the two, mount a stile **C** and drop right off the embankment to a track. Cross and walk away on a field track, shortly going over a ditch to swing beside it. Ignore the first bridge that you come to at the field corner, continuing to a second one a little farther on **D**. A path heads left between the fields towards houses grouped around a low hill. Later meeting a track, wind left and right to climb on with the hedge on your right. Leaving at the top, walk behind houses and a playing field before emerging

in Alderton. *If you wish to stop for refreshment, the village inn, **The Swan**, is a few steps to the left, otherwise continue the walk by turning right up Hollesley Road.*

After almost $^{1}/_{2}$ mile turn right **E** to follow a farm lane signed to Buckanay Farm. Keep with the tarmac past a cottage and then later, the farm buildings. Where it subsequently swings right, go ahead across a narrow field and a drainage ditch to regain the flood wall **B**. Retrace your steps across the grazing and past the Martello tower, returning to the coastguard cottages, either on the beach or along the road. ●

SCALE 1:25 000 or 2½ INCHES to 1 MILE 4CM to 1KM

walk 7

Start
Ixworth

Distance
5 miles (8km)

Height gain
100 feet (30m)

Approximate time
2½ hours

Route terrain
Bridleways, quiet lanes

P **Parking**
Car park opposite the church

OS maps
Landranger 155 (Bury St Edmunds), Explorers 211 (Bury St Edmunds & Stowmarket) and 229 (Thetford Forest in The Brecks)

GPS waypoints
- TL 932 703
- Ⓐ TL 931 706
- Ⓑ TL 914 707
- Ⓒ TL 911 702
- Ⓓ TL 937 688

Pakenham Mills from Ixworth

This short and easy route uses bridleways and quiet lanes around Ixworth in mid-Suffolk. It takes in the lovely windmill and watermill belonging to the neighbouring parish of Pakenham before returning to the village whose attractive High Street has old inns and houses.

The village hall car park is opposite the church at the southern end of Ixworth. Turn right from the car park and then left opposite **The Pykkerell Inn**, down Commister Lane. Around a bend, take the bridleway on the left almost opposite Abbey Close Ⓐ, which runs on a causeway past the grounds of Ixworth Abbey.

The house takes its name from the Augustinian priory that was built on the site in 1170. The present house incorporates much of the fabric of the monastery, including a Norman undercroft. The ditches on either side of the causeway were probably monks' fish ponds.

Cross the River Black Bourn at Hempyard Bridge and keep ahead on a field track towards a small wood. It bends right in front of the trees, later running beside a hedge. At the end of a hedgerow go left Ⓑ onto a grass track. Bear left again at the next corner across the ditch and follow it past a clump of trees, where the lack of a hedgerow opens a panoramic vista.

Turn left when faced by a metal gate Ⓒ along a farm track, Heath Lane. Beyond Gameclose Covert, views open up to Ixworth, while on the low hill in front, Pakenham windmill comes into sight. Keep ahead to the main A143 and continue up the hill along Cutter's Lane opposite. There was a sizeable Roman fort at Ixworth that covered seven acres and the lane across the top follows the line of a Roman road, which ran past it to The Wash.

Carry on along Thieves Lane beside the black-tarred Pakenham windmill, which is five storeys high and was built in 1816. It is still fully operational and can be viewed at certain times; enquire at the farm. The lane drops to Fulmer Bridge where there is a scene of meadows and stream that recalls works by the artists Constable or Cotman. Now called Broadway, the lane continues to a T-junction Ⓓ. Go left and then shortly, left again, winding through the hamlet past a tiny Methodist chapel to the beautiful Pakenham watermill. There

Farm

Ixworth
Mill

Clay Lane **71**

Potter's
Plantation

Long
Carr

B

Co Const Bdy

92

Remains of
Priory
(Augustinian)

Moat

93

PO

Cemy

Sch

Ixworth

School

48

94

Crow

C

Gameclose
Covert

7 P

A 1008

ROMAN

Bridge Farm

70

The Black Bourn

Mickle Mere

Ppg Sta

Resr

Sto

Heath Lane

A 143

Great
Queach

Mill
Cottages

Mill
Farm

Windmill

Watermill
Ford

Baileypool Lane

Queach Farm

Cutter's Lane

ROMAN ROAD (course of)

Thieves Lane

Fulmer
Bridge

Broadway

Pit (dis

Bailey

G

The
Plains

ROMAN ROAD (course of)

69

Shortbrakes MS

D W

Old Hall

Pit
(dis

SCALE 1:25000 or 2½ INCHES to 1 MILE 4CM to 1KM

0   200   400   600   800 METRES   1   KILOMETRES
                                        MILES
0   200   400   600 YARDS   ½

has been a mill on the site since at least the year 1086 and, like the windmill seen earlier, this 18th-century mill has been restored to working order. It is open to the public on Thursdays and weekends during the summer.

Mickle Mere, a small wetland nature reserve, can be seen to the right as the lane then approaches the main road. Turn left along the pavement, crossing after 50 yds at a white post to a byway on the other side. Follow it left and then right at Mill Road West to return to the starting point opposite Ixworth church. ●

Pakenham Watermill

Covehithe and Benacre

Start
Covehithe

Distance
5½ miles (8.9km)

Height gain
100 feet (30m)

Approximate time
2½ hours

Route terrain
Shingle, quiet lanes, woodland tracks

Parking
Along the lane towards Southwold from junction near church

Dog friendly
On leads through Benacre Broad nature reserve

OS maps
Landranger 156 (Saxmundham), Explorer 231 (Southwold & Bungay)

GPS waypoints
TM 521 818
Ⓐ TM 524 810
Ⓑ TM 533 838
Ⓒ TM 518 841
Ⓓ TM 512 831
Ⓔ TM 512 822

The delightful shoreline part of the route has a desert island feel to it as it passes the lagoon-like Benacre Broad, but may not be passable at exceptional tides. Elsewhere the walking is easy on quiet lanes and a woodland track. As the route passes through a Suffolk Wildlife Trust Reserve, dogs should be kept on the lead.

In its prime Covehithe was a busy port, hence the erstwhile magnificence of its church which would have rivalled that of Blythburgh. Although Cromwell has been blamed for its ruinous state, it appears that the small thatched church built within the shell of the nave in 1672 reflects the decline of Covehithe after its medieval prosperity rather than the result of Puritan vandalism.

From the junction, walk towards the church, turning right almost immediately onto a path to Covehithe Beach. Meeting a farm track, go right, soon branching off right again onto a well-trodden path that leads to the shore by Covehithe Broad Ⓐ. Turn north along the beach *below the crumbling cliffs, which are receding faster than any others in the country and should therefore be given a wide berth to avoid falling debris.*

Approaching Benacre Broad, the skeletal remains of trees scatter the beach, uprooted as the cliffs on which they perched were undercut by the waves. The area is part of a National Nature Reserve and includes a diverse range of habitats encompassing beach, dunes, heath, broads and woodland.

Beyond the lake, you can either climb to a path above or

Covehithe cliffs

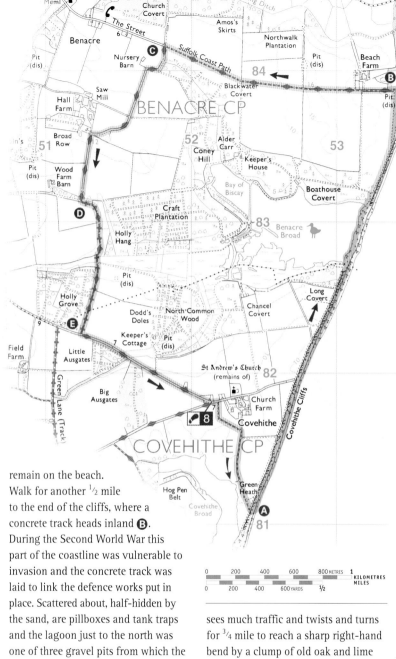

remain on the beach.
Walk for another $^1/_2$ mile
to the end of the cliffs, where a
concrete track heads inland **B**.
During the Second World War this
part of the coastline was vulnerable to
invasion and the concrete track was
laid to link the defence works put in
place. Scattered about, half-hidden by
the sand, are pillboxes and tank traps
and the lagoon just to the north was
one of three gravel pits from which the
ballast to build them was dug, the other
two having been engulfed by the sea.
Overgrowth soon narrows the broad
way to an attractive path, leading to the
entrance of the thatched Beach Farm.
Again on a track, carry on ahead
towards the tower of Benacre church,
almost hidden by trees in summer.

Reaching a lane **C**, go left. It rarely

sees much traffic and twists and turns
for $^3/_4$ mile to reach a sharp right-hand
bend by a clump of old oak and lime
trees **D**. Leave through a gate on the
left along a track signed as a byway,
shortly curving at the perimeter of a
meadow fringing Holly Hang woodland.
Carry on at the edge of another wood,
Holly Grove, to emerge onto a lane at
the far side **E**. Go left and walk the
pleasant $^1/_2$ mile or so back to the
starting point.

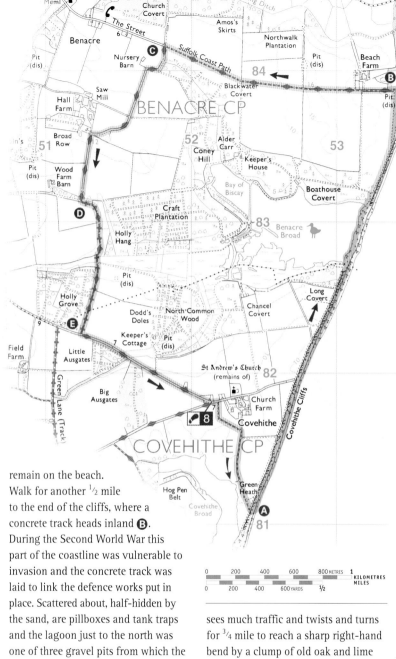
SCALE 1:25000 or 2½ INCHES to 1 MILE 4CM to 1KM

walk 9

Start
Oak Corner, Cretingham

Distance
5 miles (8km)

Height gain
215 feet (65m)

Approximate time
2½ hours

Route terrain
Bridleways, wooded paths and fields

P Parking
Street parking in village is limited, but walkers patronising The Bell may use its car park

Dog friendly
On leads through Chestnut Tree Farm at **G**

OS maps
Landranger 156 (Saxmundham), Explorer 212 (Woodbridge & Saxmundham)

GPS waypoints
☑ TM 227 603
Ⓐ TM 227 608
Ⓑ TM 242 608
Ⓒ TM 243 611
Ⓓ TM 246 613
Ⓔ TM 251 604
Ⓕ TM 249 594
Ⓖ TM 241 595
Ⓗ TM 233 598

Cretingham and Brandeston

The beautiful countryside of the Deben valley around the villages of Cretingham, Brandeston, Monewden and Hoo is particularly appealing to walkers with its excellent network of footpaths and bridleways. The small villages are virtually unspoilt and several have excellent pubs.

☑ The magnificent oak tree opposite **The Bell** is the starting point of the walk. Follow the village street towards Earl Soham past the post office and the church. Much of the church building dates from c 1300, but there were alterations and additions in the later Perpendicular style. The 14th-century porch leads through to an 18th-century interior, when each family was segregated within their own box pew and the priest delivered his sermon from the commanding triple-decker pulpit, crowned by a tester that echoed his voice around the nave. Above is a fine hammerbeam roof, its weight producing a decided lean in the north wall. There are several memorials to a branch of the Cornwallis family, who lived here in the early 17th century, and the finely carved medieval font still bears traces of its original paint.

Cross the little River Deben and turn right at the T-junction. After 100 yds, where the road bends left, keep ahead along a driveway to Cretingham Golf Club Ⓐ. Keep right as it splits, passing a pond before reaching the car park. Walk left in front of the clubhouse to a junction and turn right along a wooded sandy path across the course. Over a bridge pass through a wood and carry on beside fields to a lane. Turn right and then immediately left into a cul-de-sac signed as a bridleway Ⓑ.

After the thatched Grove Farm, with its decorative plasterwork known as pargeting, but before a red brick cottage, the bridleway swings off right Ⓒ on a broad grassy track. Turn left when you reach a narrow lane and then right after 200 yds just before The Bungalow Ⓓ. A field-edge path takes you the short distance to Mutton Lane. Go right and follow it into Brandeston by **The Queen's Head** pub.

Turn left to a junction with another road coming from Cretingham. Go right beside the triangular green, crossing the road to a bridleway opposite Ⓔ. This track descends gently to the river, giving glimpses of the church and Brandeston Hall to

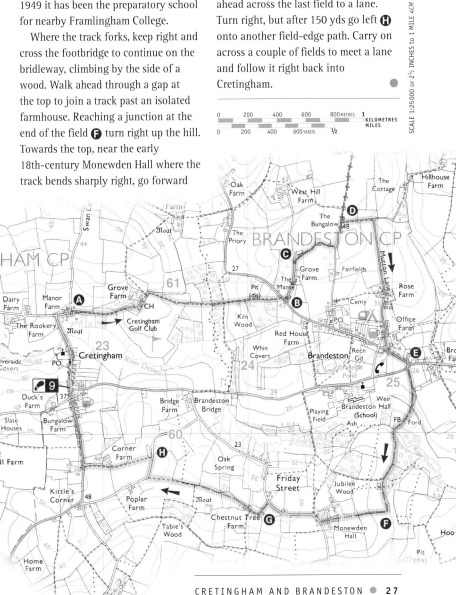

Ford across the River Deben

the right. The present mock-Tudor house of 1864 replaces an Elizabethan mansion built by Andrew Revett. Since 1949 it has been the preparatory school for nearby Framlingham College.

Where the track forks, keep right and cross the footbridge to continue on the bridleway, climbing by the side of a wood. Walk ahead through a gap at the top to join a track past an isolated farmhouse. Reaching a junction at the end of the field **F** turn right up the hill. Towards the top, near the early 18th-century Monewden Hall where the track bends sharply right, go forward

across an uncultivated corner below an ash tree. Pass through a gap in a fence and across a lawn, walking out between stables to a lane. Turn right onto the lane, leaving after $\frac{1}{4}$ mile along a track on the left to Chestnut Tree Farm **G**.

Wind through the farmyard and then follow the right-hand edge of a field towards a wood. The path skirts its perimeter and continues as a field-edge path. Shortly before Poplar Farm, the hedge swings right. However, keep ahead across the last field to a lane. Turn right, but after 150 yds go left **H** onto another field-edge path. Carry on across a couple of fields to meet a lane and follow it right back into Cretingham.

SCALE 1:25000 or 2½ INCHES to 1 MILE 4CM to 1KM

0	200	400	600	800 METRES	1
					KILOMETRES
					MILES
0	200	400	600 YARDS	½	

Start

Forest Lodge Picnic Site, West Stow

Distance

5¼ miles (8.4km)

Height gain

115 feet (35m)

Approximate time

2½ hours

Route terrain

Riverside paths, forest tracks and bridleway

P Parking

Car park at start

OS maps

Landranger 144 (Thetford & Diss), Explorer 229 (Thetford Forest in The Brecks)

GPS waypoints

TL 815 714
Ⓐ TL 814 718
Ⓑ TL 828 721
Ⓒ TL 837 720
Ⓓ TL 834 712
Ⓔ TL 821 705
Ⓕ TL 816 703

Forest and riverside from West Stow

This short walk in the Breckland of north Suffolk displays a wide variety of scenery: forest, farmland and the parkland surrounding Culford School, closing with a short length along the footpath beside the northern bank of the River Lark.

West Stow lies on the fringe of the East Anglian Brecklands, a large area cleared for agriculture during the Stone Age, but abandoned to grazing after the sandy soils lost their fertility. The present forests date from the early 20th century, when large areas of poor land were put to forest.

From the car park entrance turn left past black wooden huts. Follow a sandy forest track for 350 yds to a junction Ⓐ. Turn off right onto a narrower path threading through the fringe of the forest with open fields to the right. When the path later swings left, keep ahead out of the trees, negotiating a barbed wire barrier designed to keep stock in the fields rather than people out. Continue forward on a farm track through a meadow towards tiny Wordwell church. Passing into another field, the track curves left in front of the pink-washed Wordwell Hall. Follow the drive right to a lane Ⓑ.

Cross to the track opposite and head straight out over the fields to Blake's Spinney. Pass through the trees and continue beyond at the field edge to a junction with the Icknield Way Path Ⓒ. This long-distance trail follows the line of a prehistoric trackway that pre-dates the Peddars Way and runs down the chalky spine of southern England from the north Norfolk coast to Avebury on the Wiltshire downs.

Turn right, the dead straight track eventually emerging onto a lane at Brockley Corner. Go right for about 125 yds, taking

The lake at Culford

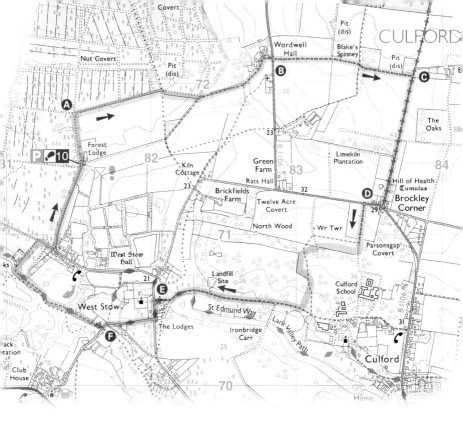

SCALE 1:25000 or 2½ INCHES to 1 MILE 4CM to 1KM

care along the road verge, to a junction with a straight cross-field track **D**. Turn left along the track, making for the woodland corner ahead. Pass through a gap and continue around the field edge at the next corner to meet a crossing track, leading to a water tower. Over the track, pass diagonally left into the trees on a narrower path, emerging at a fence corner in the grounds of Culford School. Keeping the fence on the right, walk the perimeter of the playing fields to reach the school drive opposite the cricket pitch. Go right, shortly passing, a graceful iron bridge and then an ornamental lake.

Just before reaching the end of the lake, fork off right on a waymarked path **E** that leads out to a lane opposite West Stow church. Go left, shortly taking the first right towards Flempton and walking down as far as a bridge over the River Lark **F**.

Leave right immediately before it onto the Lark Valley Path, a 13-mile route that follows the course of the River Lark from Mildenhall to Bury St Edmunds. This section is a birdwatcher's delight for it runs along a raised bank between the river and flooded pools. Reedbeds and overhanging willows provide nesting cover for waterbirds and there is always the chance of spotting a heron or even a kingfisher.

After crossing the Culford Culvert, a broader path develops that ushers you away from the river. Bend right in front of a clump of oak and then curve left beside a plantation of pine, before long passing behind foresters' cottages to reach a lane at the edge of West Stow. Go right, but in a few yards take the first turning on the left, a broad track that leads back to the starting point at the Forest Lodge Picnic Site. ●

Eye and Braiseworth

 Start

Eye

Distance

5 miles (8km).
Shorter version
2½ miles (4km)

Height gain

150 feet (45m).
Shorter version -
negligible

Approximate time

2½ hours

Route terrain

Meadow paths,
farmland tracks and
bridleways

P Parking

Buckshorn Lane car
park

OS maps

Landrangers 144
(Thetford & Diss) and
156 (Saxmundham),
Explorer 230 (Diss &
Harleston)

GPS waypoints

TM 145 738
Ⓐ TM 151 738
Ⓑ TM 152 736
Ⓒ TM 146 728
Ⓓ TM 140 710
Ⓔ TM 135 713
Ⓕ TM 140 721
Ⓖ TM 143 730

Eye, stranded away from main roads, is a charming town, the tower of its church justly described as one of the wonders of Suffolk. The heart of the town contains many interesting old buildings, including the timber-framed guildhall, all overlooked by the scanty remains of a castle, to which there is a path signed from the car park. The surrounding countryside is attractive with the diminutive River Dove having its source close to the town.

Turn left out of the car park by the library and walk to the end of Buckshorn Lane, passing a succession of pleasant cottages. Go left again below Castle Hill to reach the church.

No visitor to Eye should leave the town without seeing the church. Though the 101-ft (31m) tower is its most spectacular and lavish feature, the interior is hardly less impressive, with a beautifully restored rood screen on which painted panels depict saints and kings. The early 16th-century half-timbered guildhall stands close to the church, its woodwork richly ornamented with carvings.

Follow the main road past the south side of the church and cross the lovely River Dove by Abbey Bridge. The name refers to the Benedictine monastery that once stood on the east bank of the river. The fish ponds survive but little else. Immediately after the bridge turn right Ⓐ along Ludgate Causeway, following a sign to The Pennings, a picnic area and riverside nature reserve. Pass it and continue down the winding lane. After a left bend and a garden wall adorned with ornamental lions, turn off right onto a drive, crossing a stile by a gate into the field behind Ⓑ.

Waymarked the Mid Suffolk Footpath, it runs at the edge of consecutive rough meadows to end at the B1077 beside 'Big Head', part of the Oak Sculpture Trail. Cross to Park Lane on the other side, a pleasant country track lined with sapling oaks, given in 1998 by a variety of local organisations to replace a lost hedgerow. It leads past a succession of reed-filled ponds, *shortly passing a path off on the right, which offers a short cut back to the village* Ⓒ. The route, however, continues along the track, bearing left at a fork to rise gently onto the higher ground at the edge of the valley. Keep going as it later swings right, shortly reaching Park Farm. Walk past the farmhouse and through the farmyard, leaving along a concrete track that ends between a pair of lodges at a lane.

Turn right and walk along the road for almost ³/₄ mile, taking in the fine views to the right and passing Clint Farm on the left. After going beneath power lines and around a gentle curve, look for a path leaving on the right beside a hedge separating the fields **D**. Walk away with the hedge on your right, bearing right at the end across a narrow field to a footbridge spanning the River Dove. Keep on over another meadow to a stile beginning a tunnel-hedged path.

This enclosed way was once the path to St Mary's Church at Braiseworth, only the chancel of which survives. A Victorian church was built to replace it nearer to the centre of the tiny village, which incorporated the old church's best feature, an elaborately carved

doorway. Walk past the church and through the yard of Church Farm to leave along its access track. Just beyond the gate and almost opposite the abandoned Priory Cottage, turn right **E** onto a bridleway. It is known locally as Fen Lane, for it skirts the

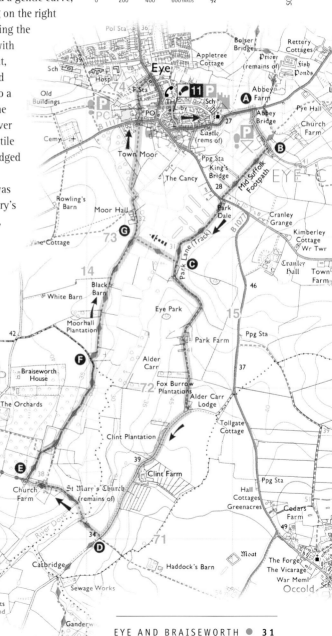

Victorian town hall in Eye

a large field towards the low remains of Black Barn at the far side.

Climb a stile by the ruin and walk on beside successive meadows, keeping a hedgerow on your left. *The short cut path from Park Lane later joins from the right by a large oak tree* **G**.

Carry on, eventually leaving the fields over a stile by Moor Hall Farm to join its driveway. After 50 yds the drive bends right. Pass through an opening on the left waymarked as a circular walk, following a ditch to a concrete bridge into woodland. Immediately within the fringe of the wood, fork right, passing a pond and before long crossing another footbridge. A little farther on go right out of the wood over a final bridge. Bear left across a recreation ground, exiting beside the community hall and changing rooms. Cross a road and walk through the old station yard, now used by a variety of light industries, keeping to the right to find a grassy path running at the edge of more woodland. Reaching the road almost opposite a row of quaint almshouses, turn right and walk up to the Victorian town hall. Just beyond, go left into Church Street and then right into Buckshorn Lane to return to the starting point.

watermeadows bordering the river.

The bridleway runs as a pleasant old track through a long line of thicket below a succession of orchards. Follow it for a little over $^1/_2$ mile then look for a waymark taking the Mid Suffolk Footpath over a stile on the right **F**. Cross the small field diagonally to a redundant stile and, entering the next meadow, go left staying close to the fence. As you head back towards Eye, there are glimpses of the distant town hall clock tower and church breaking the skyline behind the trees. Beyond a stile and plank bridge at the end of a belt of trees, keep ahead along a short boundary that sets your direction across

Framlingham and its countryside

walk 12

This pleasant walk follows paths around Framlingham Castle and out to the rural Roman Road to the north before returning alongside the River Ore. There are some outstanding views of the castle.

From the car park turn left along New Road and at the end turn left into Bridge Street. Continue up Market Hill into the town square, then turn left again into Church Street. Dedicated to St Michael, the church has a fine hammerbeam roof and several magnificent 16th and 17th century carved tombs and effigies including those of the Duke of Richmond and Henry Fitzroy, Henry VIII's illegitimate son.

Carry on past the church, but where the street turns right, keep ahead towards the castle entrance. The remains are chiefly

Start
The Elms car park, New Road, Framlingham

Distance
5½ miles (8.8km)

Height gain
165 feet (50m)

Approximate time
2½ hours

Route terrain
Field-edge paths, grassy tracks

Parking
The Elms car park

Dog friendly
Dogs on leads between Ⓓ and Ⓔ

OS maps
Landranger 156 (Saxmundham), Explorer 212 (Woodbridge & Saxmundham)

GPS waypoints
- TM 282 635
- Ⓐ TM 286 638
- Ⓑ TM 289 646
- Ⓒ TM 291 663
- Ⓓ TM 275 660
- Ⓔ TM 283 645

Leaving the pleasure garden of Framlingham Castle

Framlingham Castle

the stronghold put up by the second Earl of Norfolk between 1190 and 1210 and, unlike other East Anglian castles, there is no keep dominating the outer defence works. Now administered by English Heritage, it is well worth a visit to walk the parapet walls and climb some of the towers. It was here that Mary Tudor heard whether she or Lady Jane Grey had been declared queen after the death of Edward VI. The castle has since been used as a school, a poorhouse and a prison.

Just before reaching the moat bridge, turn left past a turnstile and then drop to cross the moat over the footbridge. Climb to a small green below the castle walls which was once a pleasure garden where the Dukes of Norfolk would sit and admire the view. Keep ahead to its far corner where a stepped path descends to a bridge spanning the ancient town ditch. Walk forward through thicket to a gate, beyond which is a junction of paths **Ⓐ**.

Bear right to follow a rising grass path into the corner of a field and continue beside its right-hand hedge. Keep ahead to a lane **Ⓑ**. Turn left and look back for a fine view of the castle.

At the junction turn right through gates towards Great Lodge Farm. Just before the farm turn left at a public footpath sign onto a gravel track that winds around the house and on between the wooded borders of fields. Turn left at the end, walk out past cottages to join a lane **Ⓒ**, and keep ahead along this Roman Road. At the T-junction bear left for 200 yds and turn right at a public footpath signposted 'Framlingham Hall Farm'. Continue along the track, which skirts the hall and its farm buildings, and then Dairy Farm, and at a junction of tracks turn left **Ⓓ**.

The permissive path continues alongside the hedge eventually reaching a footbridge beyond the end of trees. Cross and follow the River Ore left and turn the field corner to find a gap onto a lane by a public footpath sign. Rejoin the river in the field opposite and keep ahead. At its far end climb a stile into a meadow and keep ahead towards farm buildings, aiming for a stile in the top right corner of the field **Ⓔ**.

Carry on to a footbridge and then join an uphill, enclosed field edge path. Turn left at the crest, descending alongside the hedge towards

Framlingham Castle. At the bottom go left again to emerge onto a narrow lane. Turn right towards Framlingham. Beyond the left-hand playing field you can drop through a gate to follow a parallel path through The Mere Nature Reserve that offers a splendid panorama across the lake to the castle, although after wet weather, it can be muddy. The path emerges into the car park where the walk began. ●

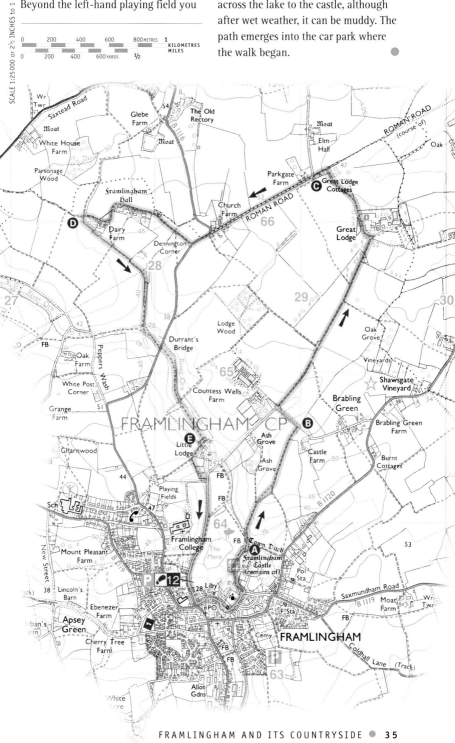

Constable Country – Flatford and East Bergholt

Start
East Bergholt

Distance
5½ miles (8.9km)

Height gain
230 feet (70m)

Approximate time
2½ hours

Route terrain
Quiet lanes, field-edge paths, paddocks

Parking
Car park at village centre

Dog friendly
On leads for much of the walk which passes grazing and wildlife areas

OS maps
Landrangers 155 (Bury St Edmunds) and 169 (Ipswich & The Naze), Explorer 196 (Sudbury, Hadleigh & Dedham Vale)

GPS waypoints

TM 069 346
Ⓐ TM 060 346
Ⓑ TM 060 343
Ⓒ TM 068 339
Ⓓ TM 067 336
Ⓔ TM 077 331
Ⓕ TM 082 331
Ⓖ TM 088 333
Ⓗ TM 086 341
Ⓙ TM 072 338

John Constable, the best-known painter of the English landscape, grew up in the lovely surroundings of the Stour valley, which forms the boundary between Suffolk and Essex. Although Constable died more than 150 years ago, much of the countryside he captured on canvas survives almost unaltered and is instantly recognisable.

Go right out of the car park past **The Red Lion** and turn right into the lane by the post office. Constable's early studio is the building on the other side of the road and belongs to the East Bergholt Society, who purchased it in 1802, 35 years before the artist's death. Pass the Congregational church and a cemetery and then, reaching a gate into Vale Farm, follow a contained path to its left, which descends to a stream and drive by a cottage. Cross and take the path climbing through a pasture on the other side. A classic view of Dedham Vale is revealed at the top, one that appeared in several of Constable's works. To the left is Dedham itself, the great tower of its church the dominating feature. Ahead is Stratford St Mary and its smaller church with the A12 beyond, a modern addition that, from here at least, hardly mars the scene.

Turn left at a footpath junction Ⓐ along a delightful sunken path. Go left again at the bottom Ⓑ onto a hedged path, which in places has more the characteristic of a wood. Reaching a green track at the end, swing right and then, in front of a gate, left, re-crossing the stream that you encountered back at Vale Farm to enter Fishpond Wood. Ignore the immediate stile and walk on a few yards within the fringe to another stile. Keep going with a hedge on your right along the lower edge of a field, crossing at the corner to continue with it now on your left. Farther on, the path becomes contained, emerging at the far end into a willow-fringed meadow. Bear left along its perimeter, leaving over a stile in the corner onto a track **G**.

Follow it right, taking the right branch signed to Flatford when it divides, to cross a tributary stream. At the next fork bear left, the footpath leading to a footbridge across the River Stour **D**. Turn left along the riverbank. This part of the route is magnificent and one of the finest riverside walks in Suffolk. All sorts of wildlife may be seen as you wander beside the water, including herons and perhaps even a kingfisher.

At length, reaching a footbridge, cross the river and walk up beside the pretty 16th-century Bridge Cottage, which houses an exhibition on Constable. Go right to pass Flatford Mill, now a field centre but once owned by Constable's father, and then Willy Lott's House, both so famously depicted in his paintings.

Bear left to pass the field centre's car park but then go right **E** onto a National Trust permissive path that takes you round the bank of a delightful pond, the habitat of a wide variety of water birds and geese. At the far end of the pond, there is a bird hide to the right overlooking the water. The route, however, goes to the left along a

SCALE 1:25 000 or 2½ INCHES to 1 MILE 4CM to 1 KM

0	200	400	600	800 METRES	1

KILOMETRES
MILES

0	200	400	600 YARDS	½

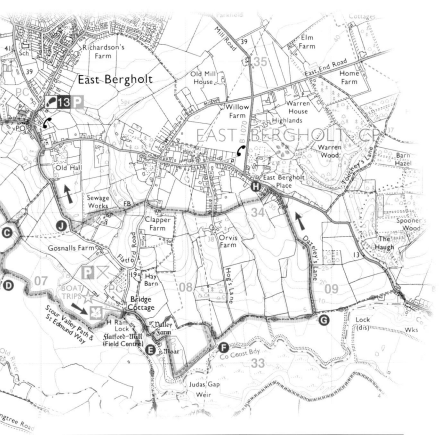

pleasant hedged track winding beside a wood. Eventually reaching a path off on the right, leave the Flatford Estate over a plank bridge into a field. Walk away by the right-hand boundary, passing beneath power cables to a stile in the corner .

Turn left to follow a hedgerow at the edge of a succession of meadows that are likely to be damp in winter. Ignore an opening on the left, the end of Hog's Lane, and keep going until you eventually reach a large wooden cattle pen. Leave the watermeadows through a gate immediately before it ⬤, climbing away along a stony track, Dazeley's Lane. Reaching a road at the top walk left, but abandon it after 50 yds, turning left again at the end of Clarence Villas ⬤ down a narrow enclosed path. Strike across a field, passing through a small thicket at the far side to another length of contained path.

Cross a track, Hog's Lane, to a footpath on the other side, following the field edge to Clapper Farm. Leave along its drive, but just before its end, the right of way cuts right over a stile and across the foot of a paddock to meet the lane from the neighbouring driveway. Opposite, the ongoing footpath falls gently beside a field to cross a stream and enter a wood. Bear left at a fork, emerging onto a grass track. Keep ahead across a final small paddock to reach another lane ⬤. Go right, initially avoiding the tarmac by using a parallel path along the bank. Continue up the lane after the two come together to a junction in front of East Bergholt church. This is worth a visit, if only to see the unique timber Bell House in the churchyard. Built after the construction of the enormous west tower was abandoned in 1525, it houses a full set of bells, which are swung by hand cranks rather than the traditional bell-ropes. Turn left into the village, passing the site of East Bergholt House, Constable's childhood home. ⬤

Flatford Mill, East Bergholt

Long Melford

Long Melford is one of the most impressive small towns in Suffolk with a long, wide main street and a beautiful green. It also has two great houses and this walk passes through the grounds of one of these, Kentwell Hall.

walk 14

Start
Long Melford

Distance
5½ miles (8.8km)

Height gain
230 feet (70m)

Approximate time
2½ hours

Route terrain
Tracks, field-edge paths

Parking
Off Church Walk

Dog friendly
Note the 'dogs on leads' signs between **B** and **C**

OS maps
Landranger 155 (Bury St Edmunds), Explorer 196 (Sudbury, Hadleigh & Dedham Vale)

GPS waypoints
TL 865 466
A TL 864 468
B TL 861 485
C TL 848 479
D TL 845 472
E TL 845 460

Turn right along Church Walk towards the church. The magnificent Holy Trinity Church is mentioned in The Buildings of England as 'one of the most moving parish churches of England, large, proud and noble'. As at Lavenham, its furnishings, monuments and architecture testify to the wealth generated by the cloth trade. Inside, the Clopton Chantry is a remarkable monument to one of the most prosperous of these medieval entrepreneurs and makes a fitting climax to visiting this outstandingly beautiful church. Beside it stands the Trinity Hospital, built and endowed by Sir William Cordell, Speaker of the House of Commons.

Continue through the churchyard and past the tower, taking the drive towards the rectory. Where it swings right, keep ahead over a stile behind a telegraph pole and follow a fence for a few paces to a squeezer stile. Cross a paddock to another squeezer stile in the far corner and pass through a belt of trees to emerge at the edge of Kentwell Park **A**.

Keep on a beaten path across the park to a stile on the far side and turn left onto an avenue of impressive limes, planted in 1678. This is the grand approach to Kentwell Hall, a moated house, which was remodelled internally after fire damage in 1822.

Bear left just before the gates to the hall following waymarkers along a track through woodland. Just in front of a wooden gate, turn right along the left-hand edge of a field, waymarked Stour Valley Path. Go through a squeezer stile and follow the track which later passes between arable fields. At a waymarked crossing of tracks turn left **B**.

A wide path follows the edge of the wood and is delightful walking. Keep left with the corner and accompany the hedge across fields, eventually reaching a waymark. Bear away from the boundary towards the foot of the field, leaving through a gap near the right corner across a plank footbridge.

Continue along the edge of a long meadow bypassing farm sheds and a yard to reach the B1066 at Cranmore Green. Follow the road right for 200 yds before turning left onto an enclosed path by Mill Farm **C**.

Cross a footbridge over the little River Glem and bear right across an arable field to another footbridge then climb ahead to meet the corner of the hedgerow. Keep ahead but after a few steps, slip through the hedge onto its other side. At the corner, go left on a grass path that swings right across another field, joining a track beside a bungalow to reach a T-junction **D**.

Turn left, cross a gravel driveway and follow posts across a wooded lawn to cross a bridge. Pass through a small thicket and carry on at the edge of a meadow to a lane.

Turn right and, at the end, cross the main road to an enclosed footpath almost opposite which climbs gradually. Maintain direction with the hedge on

Walking towards Long Melford church

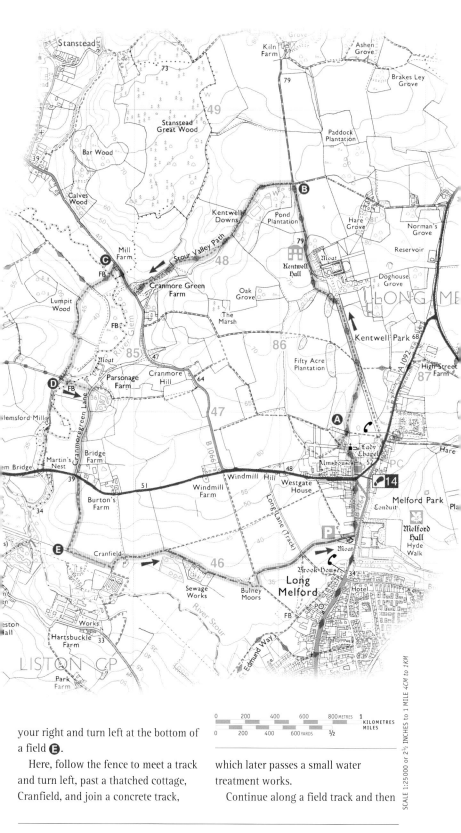

your right and turn left at the bottom of a field **E**.

Here, follow the fence to meet a track and turn left, past a thatched cottage, Cranfield, and join a concrete track, which later passes a small water treatment works.

Continue along a field track and then

Long Melford Hall

a green lane that emerges in Long Melford at the southern end of the green by an attractive, former Victorian school, now the village hall.

Turn left towards the church, past a row of elegant Georgian houses facing Melford Hall on the other side of the

main road. The hall, dating from 1559, is one of Suffolk's finest Elizabethan buildings and was also built for Sir William Cordell.

Keep ahead and cross the road, passing the **Black Lion Hotel** to return to the start of the walk

Somerleyton and Waddling Lane

Somerleyton is a splendidly eccentric village, the creation of the self-made Victorian railway magnate Sir Morton Peto, who went bankrupt in a spectacular way in 1866. Somerleyton Hall and its gardens, which include a famous maze, are open regularly in the summer. The route follows the edge of the park and returns on a lovely green way on the edge of the marshes fringing the River Waveney.

Start
The Duke's Head pub, Somerleyton

Distance
6¼ miles (10.1km)

Height gain
Negligible

Approximate time
2½ hours

Route terrain
Parkland, quiet byways

Parking
Walkers patronising The Duke's Head may use its car park. Otherwise there is street parking in the village

Dog friendly
On a lead through Kitty's Farm after Ⓑ

OS maps
Landranger 134 (Norwich & The Broads), Explorer OL40 (The Broads)

GPS waypoints
TM 478 971
Ⓐ TM 489 980
Ⓑ TM 489 982
Ⓒ TM 503 984
Ⓓ TM 498 970
Ⓔ TM 501 960
Ⓕ TM 478 967

If you begin the walk from **The Duke's Head**, look for a stone pavement block at the entrance showing that the pub lies outside the bounds of the Somerleyton estate. Turn right and follow the winding lane past neat estate cottages through the village. The Green shows these at their prettiest, with most of them thatched and the school being particularly delightful. They are contemporary with the remodelled hall and were probably by the same architect, John Thomas, who, 'discovered' by Prince Albert, achieved fame as a sculptor before taking up architecture.

Continue past the school and, when the road bends left, leave right at an Angles Way sign along the lane to Ashby beside the estate wall. Reaching a thatched lodge, turn right through a gate into the park. Follow the drive for ¼ mile to a path signed through a gap on the left Ⓐ. Head away at the field edge past a line of great oaks, the remote church of Ashby just visible through the trees ahead. Meeting a farm track Ⓑ, go right to Kitty's Farm.

Walk through the yard, winding left and right between barns. Where the track ends by a bungalow, go forward through an opening and continue along the edge of two fields. Just before the end of the second one, turn right towards a wood. Follow its boundary left, carrying on in the next field. After skirting a small pond the path enters a copse. Keep ahead within its fringe and at the edge of the subsequent field to the second of two openings on the right, partway along Ⓒ. Strike half-left across the adjacent field, making for a gap in the far hedge by a telegraph post and turn right onto Green Lane.

There follows a mile of pleasant walking along this quiet byway, from which there are glimpses to Somerleyton Hall to

Estate cottages in Somerleyton

the right. The house is Jacobean and inside are many original features such as the fabulous plaster ceiling of the ballroom, whilst other rooms reflect the later Adam style. The exterior was remodelled in 1844 and the façade is a celebration of early Victorian Anglo-Italian style. Passing Green Farm, also notice the ancient beech trees in the wood opposite. About 50 yds before meeting the busy B1074 at the end, look for a waymarked path on the left. It winds around a clump of thicket to a gate in the park wall beyond **D**. Cross to a stile opposite and walk away at the field edge. Joining a gravel track, keep ahead over a low rise, the way eventually ending through a gate onto Waddling Lane **E**.

Suffolk was famous for its turkeys and geese and the odd name for this beautiful green lane might well have come from the flocks of geese that were once driven along it to London's Smithfield Market, the geese wearing felt booties to protect their feet.

Turn right, passing after about ¼ mile a memorial on the right to an American aircrew who died during the war when their bomber crashed close to this spot. There are wide-reaching views across the flat valley of the River Waveney as you approach the fine pine trees that are a feature of the Somerleyton woodland.

Bear left when the way divides after dipping across a side valley and keep ahead when another track joins from the left. At the end, go left into Station Road. Leave opposite the station along a gravel track into a wood, shortly reaching an Angles Way sign **F**. Turn off left along a grass track into thicket, passing through a leylandii hedge into a boatyard. Bearing right, walk through to follow a track out to a lane. The Duke's Head lies just to the left. ●

SCALE 1:25000 or 2½ INCHES to 1 MILE 4CM to 1KM

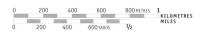

Start
Mildenhall

Distance
6¼ miles (10.1km)

Height gain
Negligible

Approximate time
2½ hours

Route terrain
Bridleway, some roads, field tracks

Parking
Jubilee Hall car park

OS maps
Landrangers 143 (Ely & Wisbech) and 154 (Cambridge & Newmarket), Explorer 226 (Ely & Newmarket)

GPS waypoints
- TL 712 744
- Ⓐ TL 700 743
- Ⓑ TL 690 743
- Ⓒ TL 676 746
- Ⓓ TL 691 738
- Ⓔ TL 702 740
- Ⓕ TL 713 739

West Row and Worlington from Mildenhall

Mildenhall lies on the edge of the Fens so the fact that there are no gradients on this walk will cause little surprise. Yet the landscape has a unique appeal for many people who enjoy walking in really open country beneath vast skies. The large church in Mildenhall is worth visiting to see its beautiful stonework, executed by masons from Ely cathedral in the 13th century, and a richly decorated hammerbeam roof. Also of interest is the museum, which has a replica of a massive silver dish, part of a Roman treasure trove found in 1943.

The Jubilee Hall car park is close to the centre of town. A path runs left from its entrance to the River Lark, which divides here to flow around Parker's Island. Go over the two bridges spanning the water to reach the south bank and turn right along the riverside path, soon emerging onto a road at Mill Bridge. Cross and drop back left to continue on the other bank past one of the town's former mills to Turf Lock. Beyond a footbridge, walk on by the river at the edge of a cricket ground and then a small wood.

Joining a bridleway, carry on to a cottage Ⓐ. Leave the track immediately after it in favour of a field-edge path beside the meandering Lark, where you might spot large fish basking in shaded pools. Over to the right Wamil Hall can be seen and then, after crossing a track by a bridge, there is a pleasing view over grazing marshes to Worlington church. Carry on along the riverbank to Kings Staunch Cottage. Pass through a kissing-gate in the high privet hedge and cross the lawn, leaving at the far side onto the edge of a field **B**. As the ongoing riverside path is generally overgrown and the Lark hidden by vegetation, it is now preferable to follow the bridleway along the top edge of the field over to the right.

After $^1/_2$ mile the path turns right to meet a lane at West Row. Go left to a bend, forking off at the second turning into Ferry Lane, which makes a wide sweep to the river at **Jude's Ferry Inn**. Cross the bridge and walk down the road for a further 200 yds before turning left **C** onto an open field track that passes one of a line of pillboxes built in the Second World War to guard the river crossing. Reaching a fork, bear left, heading towards Worlington church. At the far side of the fields, the way continues as an enclosed path to Church Farm. Bear right to the church **D** and walk through the churchyard to a gate at the eastern end. Wind around a cottage and turn off into a cemetery, following a path along its right-hand hedge. Emerging at the far end, swing left over a plank bridge and walk out to the main road.

Turn left through the village and carry on past **The Walnut Tree** pub. After $^1/_2$ mile as Mildenhall church then comes into view, look for a gated track on the right **E**. Strike out between the fields towards a wood, crossing the no-longer obvious course of an old railway line as you enter the trees. After bending left, the track swings right, but you should leave at that point, keeping ahead on a narrower path. Later breaking from the trees, there is a view to the old railway sheds and platform buildings of the former Mildenhall Station. Having broadened to a track, the way continues to a lane, which, to the right, leads to Barton Mills. Leave at the second sharp bend along a footpath on the left **F**, which runs at the edge of a small water-meadow nature reserve to the river. Retrace your outward steps over the pair of footbridges back to Jubilee Hall.

SCALE 1:25000 or 2½ INCHES to 1 MILE 4CM to 1KM

0	200	400	600	800 METRES	1 KILOMETRES MILES
0	200	400	600 YARDS	½	

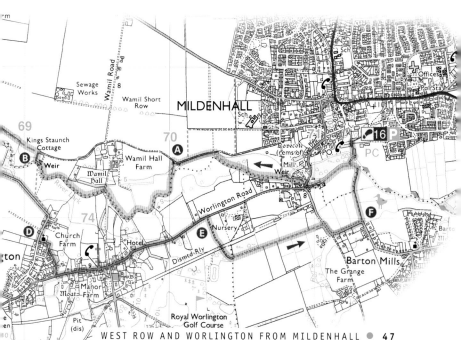

Slightly harder walks of up to 3 – 3½ hours

Orford and its castle

Orford coast and country

walk

Start
Orford

Distance
6¼ miles (10.1km)

Height gain
100 feet (30m)

Approximate time
3 hours

Route terrain
Field paths, quiet lanes

Parking
Car park on road to quay opposite Jolly Sailor inn

OS maps
Landrangers 156 (Saxmundham) and 169 (Ipswich & The Naze), Explorer 212 (Woodbridge & Saxmundham)

GPS waypoints
- TM 424 496
- Ⓐ TM 422 509
- Ⓑ TM 428 514
- Ⓒ TM 428 515
- Ⓓ TM 420 519
- Ⓔ TM 409 489

Orford is a 'must' for any visitor to Suffolk, with its polygonal Norman castle and a large church that had its origins in the same age. Its importance at this time was as a port, but like so many of Suffolk's havens it began to silt up, so Defoe wrote in 1722: 'The sea daily throws up more land so it is a sea port no longer'. The walk covers field paths, lanes and the flood wall facing the River Ore, which is a popular summer walk.

Turn right out of the car park to walk up Orford's attractive main street towards the church. St Bartholomew's dates from 1166 and is contemporary with the castle, although only the ruined chancel arches remain from the original building. In the 14th century, when the place developed as a thriving seaport, the church was rebuilt and the tower added, but part of this subsequently collapsed in 1830. Amongst its treasures is a splendid font with an inscription begging prayers for the departed and also some fine brasses. In its medieval heyday Orford had two other churches plus a friary and two hospitals, their memory retained in the names of Chantry Farm and Chantry Marshes to the south.

Walk through the churchyard to avoid a dangerous corner, emerging opposite the square beside **The King's Head**. The castle lies beyond the far end of the square, the top of the keep giving a wonderful panorama of the countryside covered by the walk. It was built by Henry II in the 12th century to defend the coast. The route, however, continues to the right, turning right again into Ferry Road towards Iken. Keep ahead for ½ mile to reach an electricity sub-station, opposite which a bridleway is signed through the hedge Ⓐ. Strike out across a field, joining the left hedge at the far end. Leave through a gate in the corner and go right and then immediately left along a field track. After some 300 yds, as an isolated brick building comes into view ahead, look for a waypost Ⓑ.

Bear left up the banking and cut across the field to the end of a hedge. Walk on through a gate beside the hedge to another gate Ⓒ. Turn through it and climb upfield to a gate near the top corner. Bear right across the next field, making for a kissing-gate towards the middle of the top hedge. Cross a lane

The River Ore

track swings to the left, ultimately ending at a lane. Go right and after almost ¹⁄₄ mile turn left onto a hedged track **E**.

It drops onto the reclaimed salt marshes, making for the distant flood bank ahead. Climb onto the wall and turn left along the top, following the sinuous course of the River Ore. This is a wonderful place to watch for oystercatchers and other waders as well as heron, who, as you approach, often wait until the last moment before lazily taking to their wings.

and continue on the other side, heading for the small spire of Sudbourne church, to be briefly glimpsed above trees. Joining a boundary on the right, pass the church to reach a track at the corner of the churchyard **D**.

Turn left, shortly meeting a narrow lane. The bridleway continues opposite, after a while going through the fringe of a small wood and then crossing more fields to a road. Cross to a broad track and follow it on, passing Orford Lodge and later skirting an outpost of Tunstall Forest known as Gedgrave Broom. Eventually the main

Silence is one of the great qualities here, broken only by the call of birds and rustling of the wind. Moored craft herald the end of the path, which finally drops onto the Orford waterfront. Go left up the main street back to the car park opposite **The Jolly Sailor**. ●

Terraced cottages in Orford

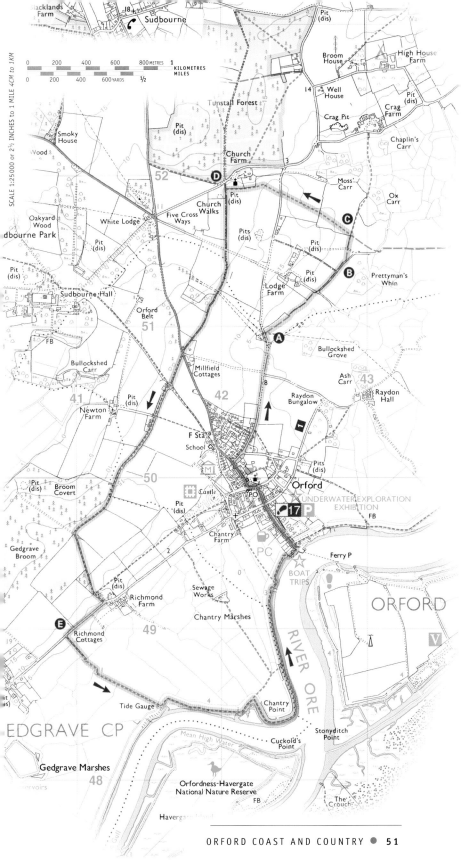

walk 18

Start

Leiston Leisure Centre (on the south east side of town)

Distance

6½ miles (10.5km)

Height gain

Negligible

Approximate time

3 hours

Route terrain

Coastal path, quiet lane, broad tracks

Parking

Car park at start

OS maps

Landranger 156 (Saxmundham), Explorer 212 (Woodbridge & Saxmundham)

GPS waypoints

- TM 451 619
- **A** TM 462 622
- **B** TM 471 622
- **C** TM 473 594
- **D** TM 471 597
- **E** TM 462 598
- **F** TM 459 600
- **G** TM 456 606
- **H** TM 458 612

Thorpeness from Leiston

On this exploration of the coast and heathland between Leiston and Thorpeness there is much beautiful countryside to be enjoyed. The Meare, an enormous boating lake, and the famous House in the Clouds and windmill are attractions that will appeal to children.

Leaving the Leisure Centre, turn left along Grimsey's Lane. It soon degrades to an unsurfaced track and leads to Crownlands Cottage ⅓ mile away, where it crosses the course of a former branchline that connected Aldeburgh to the main line at Saxmundham. The railhead is just to the north and now serves the Sizewell atomic power stations that loom ahead.

Go forward at a junction before a cottage and continue between open fields, swinging left at the far side towards a house. Just before it **A**, a path leads away to the right, passing beneath power cables and shortly reaching a five-way junction. Ignoring the immediate field opening, turn left just beyond it onto a hedged bridleway. Approaching its end as Home Farm becomes visible through the hedge, low posts mark a path leaving on the right **B**. An indistinct trod forks across the heath, cutting the corner to reach a lane by the entrance of Sizewell Hall.

Cross to follow a driveway to Cliff House Caravan Park, continuing ahead on a contained path that leads to the coast. Turn right along the top of the sandy cliffs past Sizewell Hall, today run as a Christian residential centre. A tunnel takes you below its terrace that overlooks the beach. Keep going alongside the perimeter wall of Dower House where, looking back on a clear day, you might see the Southwold lighthouse. Eventually reaching a gate into the private grounds of Ness House, the path slopes down to continue at the head of the shingle beach around Thorpe Ness, where Aldeburgh comes into view ahead.

Beyond soft, crumbling cliffs, you can abandon the beach for the village streets or remain on the shore as far as a wooden walkway leading off the beach **C**. Walk through to a track, going right and left to a junction beside **The Beach House** coffee shop. Follow the road right, towards Aldringham past the lake and golf club entrance. **The Dolphin Inn** lies at the top of

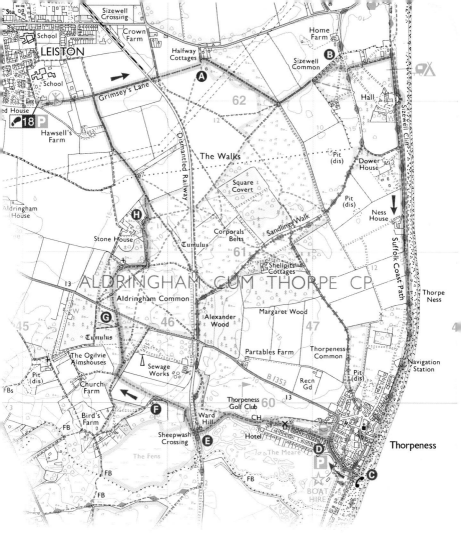

the road, but the walk leaves before then along Uplands Road on the left **D**.

Built in 1910 as a holiday retreat, the village contains some remarkable architecture that includes a church, country club and almshouses as well as numerous cottages. The dominant building at its centre is a massive water tower that looks more like the gatehouse to an Oxbridge college, while the golf clubhouse and boathouse fronting the 65-acre (26ha) artificial lake known as The Meare are equally eye-catching.

Uplands Road leads past wooden chalets to the House in the Clouds (a former water tower in disguise) and a post mill, brought here to pump well water up to a storage tank atop the tower. Beyond a car park, keep ahead on a waymarked path past the clubhouse, another striking building having towers each topped by four oversized nailheads. Continue at the edge of woodland fringing the golf course, later curving around beside a strip of water that is part of The Meare.

Emerging beside a cottage at Sheepwash Crossing **E** walk forward over the disused trackbed to find a contained path opposite that swings right behind a former railway building. The marsh to the left is the North Warren Nature Reserve, created in 1939 as the first RSPB reserve. The path winds into trees, before long crossing a boardwalk spanning a boggy stream *(be careful in wet weather for the planks may be slippery)* to reach a small fenced enclosure. Following a waymark, bear right at the edge of a garden area to a power cable post and pass through a tree fringe to the edge of a field **F**. Go left, heading across the field to a stile at the far side. Walk out to a surfaced track, which to the right eventually leads to a lane **G**.

Cross to a footpath opposite and strike across gorse heath. Keep going forward when you meet a crossing path to find a broad track, which to the right passes a former Baptist chapel. Winding at the edge of a wood beyond, it leads to a row of cottages. Carry on past the frontage and along a grass track **H** skirting the corner of a golf course. Twisting right to meet another path, turn left across the heath, shortly joining a track that continues at the edge of fields. Maintaining direction, it later leads beneath power cables and then, becoming enclosed between hedges, finally returns you to Grimsey's Lane. The Leisure Centre is then a little way to the left. ●

Thorpeness post mill

Saxmundham, Kelsale and the Gull Stream

walk 19

Start
Saxmundham

Distance
7 miles (11.3km)

Height gain
215 feet (65m)

Approximate time
3 hours

Route terrain
Field-edge paths, narrow lanes

Parking
Car park adjacent to Saxmundham station

OS maps
Landranger 156 (Saxmundham), Explorer 212 (Woodbridge & Saxmundham)

GPS waypoints
- TM 386 632
- **A** TM 380 638
- **B** TM 380 641
- **C** TM 371 645
- **D** TM 365 663
- **E** TM 383 656
- **F** TM 396 650
- **G** TM 392 639

In many Suffolk villages, 'gull' refers to a watercourse that is mostly dry but takes storm water after heavy rain. Such is the case with Gull Stream at Saxmundham and this walk follows it to the lakes that are its source, exploring some beautiful countryside before returning via Kelsale, where the church has a very unusual lychgate.

From the car park entrance, go left and left again to walk beneath the railway bridge. Pass the road to Framlingham, but just before Fairfield Drive, turn left onto a track, Harpers Lane. By a thatched lodge it narrows, swinging right to a housing estate. Keep ahead along Henley Close past a junction, leaving right just before bollards onto a path between houses. Over a footbridge, wind left and right to meet another street by a school. Cross to the ongoing path, which leads up to a playing field. Bear left across, passing left of a sunken play area to reach a stile **A**.

Turn right along the field edge, curving left at the bottom past the tiny Church of St Peter with its tower of red brick dating from the 16th century. Carlton Hall, until recently a sad and extensive ruin, has been restored and stands behind the church in what was once an extensive park. When the grass track swings right **B**, keep ahead beside a hedged ditch containing Gull Stream, a tributary of Saxmundham's River Fromus.

Pass through a clump of trees and carry on beside the stream, ignoring a crossing path and eventually climbing to a busy main road. Cross to the path opposite, which alternates through thicket and beside fields, in time reaching a lane by Vale Farm.

Turn left, but after 100 yds and just before a cottage on the left, leave through an opening on the right **C**. A pleasant field path meanders beside a wood and the Gull Stream, which, true to its nature rarely contains much water in the summer months. The path ultimately leads into Lakeside Leisure Park. Joining a drive, follow it right and then left, keeping ahead at a T-junction up to the bottom lake. Swing left along its bank and continue beside a second pool. At the top, bear left to a driveway and turn right, following it out to a quiet lane. Walk left for almost $\frac{1}{2}$ mile to a sharp bend, abandoning it there for a broad track on the right 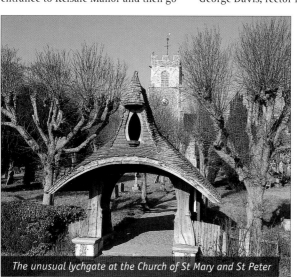D.

It runs across the fields, winding past the site of Sparkes Farm, now reduced to hardstandings. Continue along the track until it is closed by gates. Cross a footbridge through the hedge on the right and climb away at the edge of a paddock. Carry on beside a second enclosure, swinging right at the top corner into a crop field. Walk past a field access and then bear left into the corner of a scrub wood, looking for a plank bridge leading out on the right. Turn left along the field edge beside the wood. The path later slips through the hedge to join a track which, to the right, eventually passes Hall Farm to end on the main road.

Cross to a path on the other side, which rises over a high embankment onto a narrow lane. Go left to the B1121 at Dorley's Corner, crossing to a field entrance opposite the junction E. Walk forward and then bear right beside the ditch, leaving at the far end onto a narrow lane. Turn right passing the entrance to Kelsale Manor and then go left up a stepped path to the churchyard.

The church, dedicated to St Mary and St Peter, is mentioned in the Domesday Book, and Norman detail on the north doorway confirms its age. However, it has been altered over the centuries, most significantly with a large nave being added alongside the original in the 14th century. The Victorian restoration was overseen by E S Prior in the Arts and Crafts style and particularly interesting are the windows, which include work by William Morris, Sir Edward Burne-Jones and Ford Madox Brown. Perhaps the most striking feature is the unusual, but charming lychgate. Also by Prior, it stands to the memory of the Reverend George Davis, rector from 1868 until 1894, who, to quote the church guide, 'transformed this village church into a 19th-century design centre'.

Leave through the lychgate and follow the street down into the village. Turn left at the bottom and later fork right onto Lowes Hill. Some 200

The unusual lychgate at the Church of St Mary and St Peter

SCALE 1:25000 or 2½ INCHES to 1 MILE 4CM to 1KM

| 0 | 200 | 400 | 600 | 800 METRES | 1 |
| 0 | 200 | 400 | 600 YARDS | ½ | KILOMETRES MILES |

yds after crossing the railway look for a signed path on the right **F**. Over a plank bridge and through thicket, walk away at the field edge. Crossing a grass track from The White House, keep ahead with the hedgerow now on your left until you reach a lane. Turn right, but after ¼ mile go left, striking across the field

to a railway embankment **G**.

Follow the branch line, which serves the Sizewell power station, right to its junction with the main line from Great Yarmouth to Ipswich. Over stiles cross the double track and go left beside it. Continue at the edge of a small meadow and along a final stretch of path to meet the road next to the railway bridge in Saxmundham. Turn beneath it to return to the starting point.   ●

SAXMUNDHAM, KELSALE AND THE GULL STREAM ● 57

Lavenham and Brent Eleigh

Start

Lavenham

Distance

7¼ miles (11.6km)

Height gain

230 feet (70m)

Approximate time

3½ hours

Route terrain

Quiet lanes, bridleways, disused railway track and field-edge paths

Parking

Car park opposite the church, beside The Cock pub

Dog friendly

Note the 'dogs on leads' signs between Ⓐ and Ⓑ

OS maps

Landranger 155 (Bury St Edmunds), Explorer 196 (Sudbury, Hadleigh & Dedham Vale)

GPS waypoints

🖊 TL 914 489
Ⓐ TL 919 480
Ⓑ TL 937 475
Ⓒ TL 943 488
Ⓓ TL 920 491
Ⓔ TL 910 494
Ⓕ TL 900 490
Ⓖ TL 906 488

This is a classic Suffolk walk from Lavenham, one of the country's best-preserved market towns featuring some beautiful medieval timber-framed houses and a magnificent church as well as the delightful 13th century church in nearby Brent Eleigh and its historic wall paintings.

Lavenham is a perfect English village with its array of timber-framed houses and an impressive church reflecting the great wealth generated by the medieval cloth industry. Flemish weavers settled here in the 14th century and the town developed a reputation for its 'Lavenham Blue' cloth. Much of the wool produced here was exported to Europe, Africa and Asia. The size of the 15th century church, dedicated to St Peter and St Paul, has been described as a miniature cathedral, demonstrating the town's prosperity at that time. It is said that the 141ft tower would have been

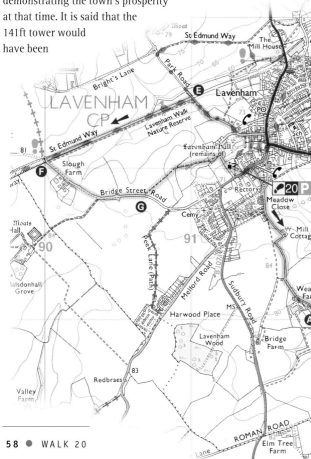

even higher had the mason not fallen from the top. Such was the trade that three separate guildhalls were built, the most notable being the Guildhall Corpus Christi overlooking the market place. Once used as a prison, workhouse, almshouse and store, it is now cared for by the National Trust and contains a fascinating exhibition describing the town's history. Here, you can also see the remains of Ramesses, a mummified cat, discovered in a nearby roof.

Leaving the car park turn right along Church Street and a few paces farther, turn right between houses (nos 32 and 34) along a narrow path. Where it ends turn right along a lane and continue past Mill Cottage to Bear's Lane Farm, turning left at a public footpath sign **A**.

Follow this enclosed path past the farm and continue along a grassy path along the left edge of a field, turning right where it reaches another field. After the path curves left, go through a hedge gap and continue to the right of a stream, later crossing an earth bridge to enter a young plantation of ash, oak, beech and maple.

The path emerges at a concrete drive. Turn right here and immediately left and continue along the left-hand field edge path, which curves right to reach Cock Lane **B**.

Turn left along the lane, which climbs and then descends to a crossroads and **The Cock** pub on the left. Cross the road

SCALE 1:25'000 or 2½ INCHES to 1 MILE 4CM to 1KM

0	200	400	600	800 METRES	1
					KILOMETRES
					MILES
0	200	400	600 YARDS	½	

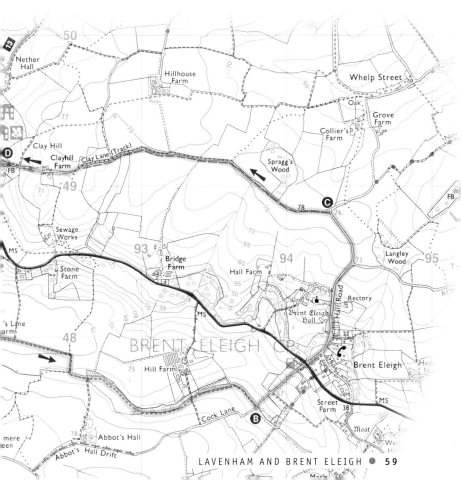

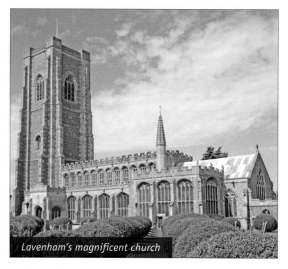
Lavenham's magnificent church

where you'll see pargeting on this building including the Tudor Rose and Fleur de Lis.

Turn left along Park Road and at a circular walk footpath sign, go through a metal gate on the left **E**. Keep along this path, St Edmund Way, which is the trackbed of an old railway line that once linked Lavenham with Sudbury. This is a popular path with birdwatchers and there are occasional seats from where you might spot woodpeckers. Over to the left there is a good view of Lavenham church. After passing under a bridge, bear right up the slope and at the top, turn right **F**.

Cross the bridge and keep ahead turning left along a grassy path at a circular walks signpost **G**.

Head across fields towards the church, go through a wooden gate and continue beside a paddock. Go through two more gates and at the road, turn right.

At the church, climb steps on the left. The crest on the church tower belongs to the de Veres or Earls of Oxford. Aubrey de Vere was granted the manor of Lavenham by his brother-in-law, William the Conqueror and 400 years later, John de Vere, the 13th Earl of Oxford, led Henry VII's army at the Battle of Bosworth in 1485. This was the final battle of the War of the Roses and local merchants built the church in thanks for his safe return and victory. Bear right through the churchyard to the road and cross this to return to the car park. ●

and keep ahead in the direction of Brent Eleigh. Cross a brick bridge – look out for kingfishers here – and continue ahead along Hall Road to St Mary's Church.

The church is well worth a visit as it contains medieval box pews and some wall paintings that remained hidden until 1960. Over the altar is one of the best-preserved pieces in England, depicting the crucifixion.

Bear left at a triangular green, continue for 400 yds and where the road swings right, turn left at a bridleway signpost **C**.

Follow the sheltered track (Clay Lane) for 1½ miles and once past Clay Hill Farm it descends to a road **D**.

Turn left and then bear right along Water Street with its fine, timber-framed houses. Look out for Lady Street on the right which leads to the Market Place and Guildhall should you wish to visit these. Since nothing took its place when the wool trade declined the town centre kept its medieval street plan and has a fine collection of crooked, half-timbered houses, many of them listed buildings.

Back to the walk, continue to the road and turn right, past **The Swan**

Sudbury and its water meadows

A varied and pleasant walk across ancient meadows beside the River Stour, along a disused railway line which is now a nature reserve and through the market town of Sudbury where the artist Gainsborough was born.

walk 21

Start
Rodbridge picnic site (off the B1064)

Distance
7½ miles (12km)

Height gain
150 feet (45m)

Approximate time
3½ hours

Route terrain
Meadows, disused railway track and town pavements

Parking
Car park at Rodbridge

Dog friendly
On lead in Sudbury meadows

OS maps
Landranger 155 (Bury St Edmunds), Explorer 196 (Sudbury, Hadleigh & Dedham Vale)

GPS waypoints
  TL 857 437
Ⓐ TL 853 430
Ⓑ TL 846 421
Ⓒ TL 850 413
Ⓓ TL 872 408
Ⓔ TL 869 413
Ⓕ TL 861 423

The wildlife haven of Rodbridge picnic site was created when gravel pits that were used to build nearby airfields during the Second World War, were flooded.

  With your back to the entrance to the car park head towards a picnic area with seats and bear right towards a wooden 'Valley Trail' signpost. Bear left and cross a road bridge and then turn left to follow the Valley Trail. At a wooden barrier, turn right and at the road, turn left and head uphill. Ignoring a public footpath sign on the left, turn left at the bridleway sign Ⓐ.

Keep to the right of a hedge and at the field corner, go through a hedge gap and then bear left, later bearing right to follow the field edge path all the way to a road. Turn left and at the junction turn left again Ⓑ.

Go across Bardfield Bridge and continue uphill. At the top turn left to join a footpath opposite Smeetham Hall Lane Ⓒ.

Bear right at the field corner and then left through a hedge gap before continuing along the path and joining a farm track. Pass a row of cottages and just after crossing a brick bridge, turn right and descend a set of wooden steps. After a few paces,

North Meadow

The statue of Thomas Gainsborough

Gainsborough. With your back to the statue, head down Market Hill past the **Black Boy** pub into Gainsborough Street and turn right into Weavers Lane. On the left is the entrance to Gainsborough's House, where the artist was born in 1727 and home to the biggest collection of his work outside of London. A few paces farther is Vanners, a silk factory that has been weaving since 1740.

Continue along Church Walk and cross the main road towards the church. Turn left and just before the fire station, go down the embankment via a set of steps to the disused railway line, where trains operated from 1865 until 1967, linking the area to Cambridge and Bury St Edmunds.

Turn left and keep ahead along a sheltered path, crossing a series of iron bridges to reach the market town of Sudbury, which flourished from its medieval cloth, and 19th century silk weaving industries.

Just before the railway walk terminates, go through a wooden barrier on the left and head through a car park **D**.

Leave the car park and bear right and at the main road turn left along Station Road. At the end, turn right, pass the library, and head towards the church in front of which is a statue of Thomas turn right into Walnut Tree Lane and pass the **Mill Hotel**. Turn right here, in front of the hotel, and in the corner turn right in front of a fence **E**.

Follow the gravel path to the left of a stream, cross the sluice and keep ahead ignoring the first wooden bridge on the right. Just before a kissing-gate turn right to cross a concrete bridge and enter North Meadow through another kissing-gate. This common land is part of 115 acres of water meadows on the flood plain of the River Stour and is an attractive area that is home to grazing cattle and crossed by many footpaths.

Continue ahead across the meadow with the River Stour to your left, go through a metal gate and over a footbridge, then cross another meadow and go through two gates. Now head for the left-hand field corner and leave the meadows through a kissing-gate. Turn left to cross a bridge and pass Brundon

Mill and its vast collection of swans. Where the tarmac drive swings left, keep ahead along the bridleway and at the next junction turn right on to the disused railway line **F**.

Follow the peaceful path for a little over ½ mile to the wooden barrier where you first left the Valley Trail and retrace your steps to the start. ●

SCALE 1:25000 or 2½ INCHES to 1 MILE 4CM to 1KM

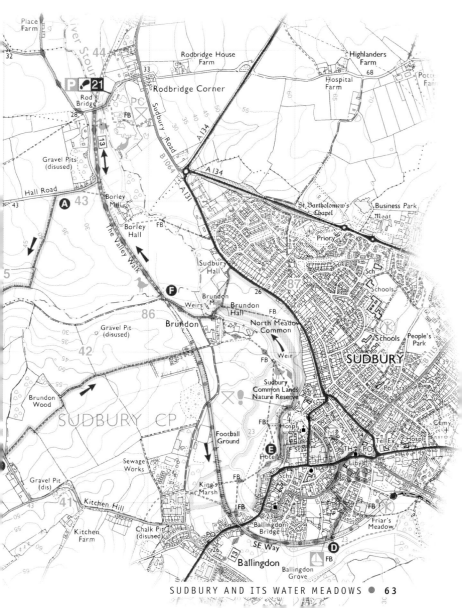

walk 22

Clare and Cavendish

Start
Clare Country Park

Distance
7½ miles (11.9km)

Height gain
310 feet (95m)

Approximate time
3½ hours

Route terrain
Field-edge paths,
tarmac drive, riverside
paths

Parking
At start

OS maps
Landranger 155 (Bury
St Edmunds), Explorers
196 (Sudbury,
Hadleigh & Dedham
Vale) and 210
(Newmarket &
Haverhill)

GPS waypoints
🏁 TL 770 451
Ⓐ TL 775 463
Ⓑ TL 798 466
Ⓒ TL 808 465
Ⓓ TL 811 460
Ⓔ TL 796 453
Ⓕ TL 775 447

The attractive villages of Clare and Cavendish both have rare character and enough antique shops to impress Lovejoy. The steep motte of Clare's Norman castle is still dominant, topped by walls of a keep, while Cavendish has a lovely green. This walk follows the Stour valley downstream to where you cross to the Essex side of the river for the return to Clare.

The pargeting on many of the houses is one of the delights of Clare. The plaster decorations, washed in pastel shades, date from the 17th century and include all kinds of designs from simple geometric shapes to intricate patterns and figures. Richard Fitzherbert, who fought with William the Conqueror at Hastings, built Clare Castle in c1090. His successors took the name de Clare and over the next two centuries, enlarged the stronghold, adding an inner and outer bailey. In 1314, the last of the de Clares was killed at the Battle of Bannockburn, and the castle subsequently deteriorated. In 1865, the Great Eastern Railway Company built a

station and goods yard within the castle bailey, part of the Stour Valley Line between Sudbury and Haverhill. It became a busy passenger and freight route, operating for more than 100 years before it closed, along with many other local branch lines. The

The Five Bells

buildings are now used by the Clare Country Park; the goods shed housing a small exhibition.

 Walk below the castle mound past the visitor centre and continue past

SCALE 1:25000 or 2½ INCHES to 1 MILE 4CM to 1KM

| 0 | 200 | 400 | 600 | 800 METRES | 1 |
| 0 | 200 | 400 | 600 YARDS | ½ | KILOMETRES MILES |

the station itself, cross a footbridge and then turn left onto a path following the castle moat. At a junction at the back of houses, turn right and follow the path to leave Clare Country Park and arrive at Cavendish Road. Go right and almost immediately left along Harp Lane, waymarked as The Stour Valley Path.

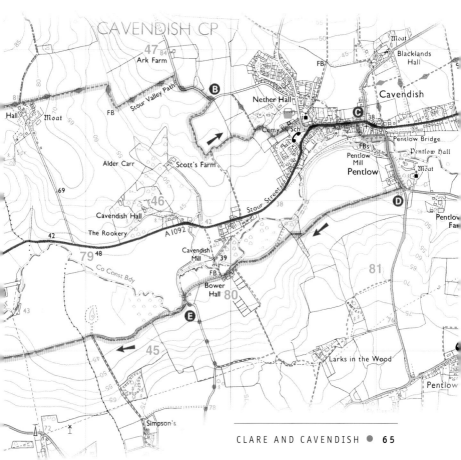

The Motte, Clare Castle country park

Beyond the police station, it degrades to a track, passing a chicken house and continuing as an enclosed path. Emerging onto the edge of a field, follow it left to the corner near Hermitage Farm Ⓐ.

Head right and climb beside the hedge, pausing to look back for a good view of Clare. Turn left at the top, go through a hedge gap and continue with the hedge on your left. After the path swings right, cross a track and keep ahead past the yard, walking in the field beyond with the boundary on your right. Halfway along, slip through a wide gap, following the other side of the hedge to the bottom of the field. Go right, reaching a footbridge on the left across the ditch, some 300 yds along. On the other bank, swing right and left over a smaller bridge to head away with the ditch on your left. Turn right onto a lane, leaving it after ¼ mile at the second left-hand bend for a footpath on the right Ⓑ.

It takes a pleasantly meandering route around field edges, eventually passing another path signed off to the right. After another 300 yds cross a plank bridge and continue on the opposite flank into the corner. Turn right over a footbridge and enter a meadow, following its boundary around left and leaving on a contained path that winds beside a cemetery to Cavendish village green by the school. Walk past the school and **The Five Bells** pub and ahead of you is the church.

The village is the 14th century ancestral home of the Cavendish family, the Dukes of Devonshire, whose family seats are at Chatsworth in Derbyshire

and Yorkshire's Bolton Abbey. Turn right at the road and at the main road, turn left to continue along the High Street. At the **Bull Inn** cross the road and leave the High Street along a gravel driveway, at a public footpath signpost **C**.

The path veers left in front of a house and at a public footpath sign turn right to walk between houses. At a stream turn left and follow the waymarked path, shortly crossing a footbridge to the right, then climb a stile to enter a meadow. Turn left to walk on the right hand side of a row of poplar trees, to a stile. Turn right at the road and continue ahead and at a junction, turn sharp right along a bridleway **D**.

The bridleway runs away at the field edge along the valley of the meandering River Stour. After a while it passes through thicket and then beside open fields once more, eventually reaching Bower Hall. Beyond, the way, becomes metalled and before long leads to a pumping station by a bend **E**. Turn off to the right here onto a wooded bridleway above the river, keeping ahead when it later emerges at the edge of successive fields. The track eventually swings right towards the river, meeting a gravel track. Follow it left to a road and there go right. After 200 yds look for a signed path on the right **F**.

Walk down to a footbridge over the River Stour and then head left towards the far corner. Cross an overflow weir and continue beside the channel passing the former mill. Reaching the old girder railway bridge, cross back to the starting point. ●

walk 23

Iken and Tunstall Forest

Start

The Pines car park at the rear of the concert hall, Snape Maltings

Distance

7¾ miles (12.3km)

Height gain

150 feet (45m)

Approximate time

3½ hours

Route terrain

Reed edge and estuary paths, forest tracks

Parking

The Pines car park, Snape Maltings. If busy in summer, alternative start at Iken Cliff picnic site Ⓐ

OS maps

Landranger 156 (Saxmundham), Explorer 212 (Woodbridge & Saxmundham)

GPS waypoints

⬛ TM 393 573
Ⓐ TM 401 562
Ⓑ TM 411 560
Ⓒ TM 411 551
Ⓓ TM 406 547
Ⓔ TM 401 542
Ⓕ TM 385 562

The ingredients of this walk are simple: an outward leg on a path along the shore of a reed-fringed estuary, the return on a forest track. The area is linked to Benjamin Britten whose music captures its atmosphere perfectly and there's much to explore at the start itself including the ancient bridge and the Maltings, which has been transformed into one of Europe's best concert venues.

From the information board beside a bench overlooking the reed beds, go down the adjacent steps and turn right to arrive at a path junction beside a waymarked post. Turn left to join the Suffolk Coast Path and head towards marshland.

A plank walk and a footbridge takes the path across the head of a creek. After this you may like to divert onto a path that sweeps left through coastal grassland which, as the notice says, is an ideal spot for a picnic. Both paths come together farther on, continuing along another stretch of boardwalk as Iken church comes into view across the reed beds and a bend of the river. Keep going, eventually passing

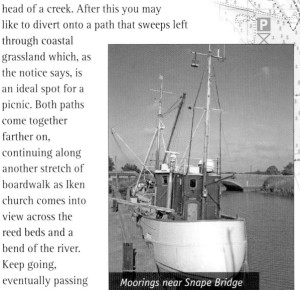

Moorings near Snape Bridge

below *Iken Cliff picnic area and car park, the alternative start if parking is congested at the Maltings.* This is a delightful spot to pause and take in the tranquil beauty of the scene. It is hard to imagine the staithe here being busy with river traffic in the 18th and 19th centuries, when grain was loaded into barges bound for London. Keep ahead following 'Suffolk Coast and Heaths Path' waymarks to reach a junction of tracks below a house **A**. Bear left along the Suffolk Coast Path past Jumbo's Cottage to join a gravel path, the way dropping to run at the edge of the marsh. Farther on the marsh gives way to a sandy beach below a low cliff, which at high water may be washed by the tide for a short time. The path eventually climbs over the flood embankment and through thicket, becoming enclosed to reach a lane **B**.

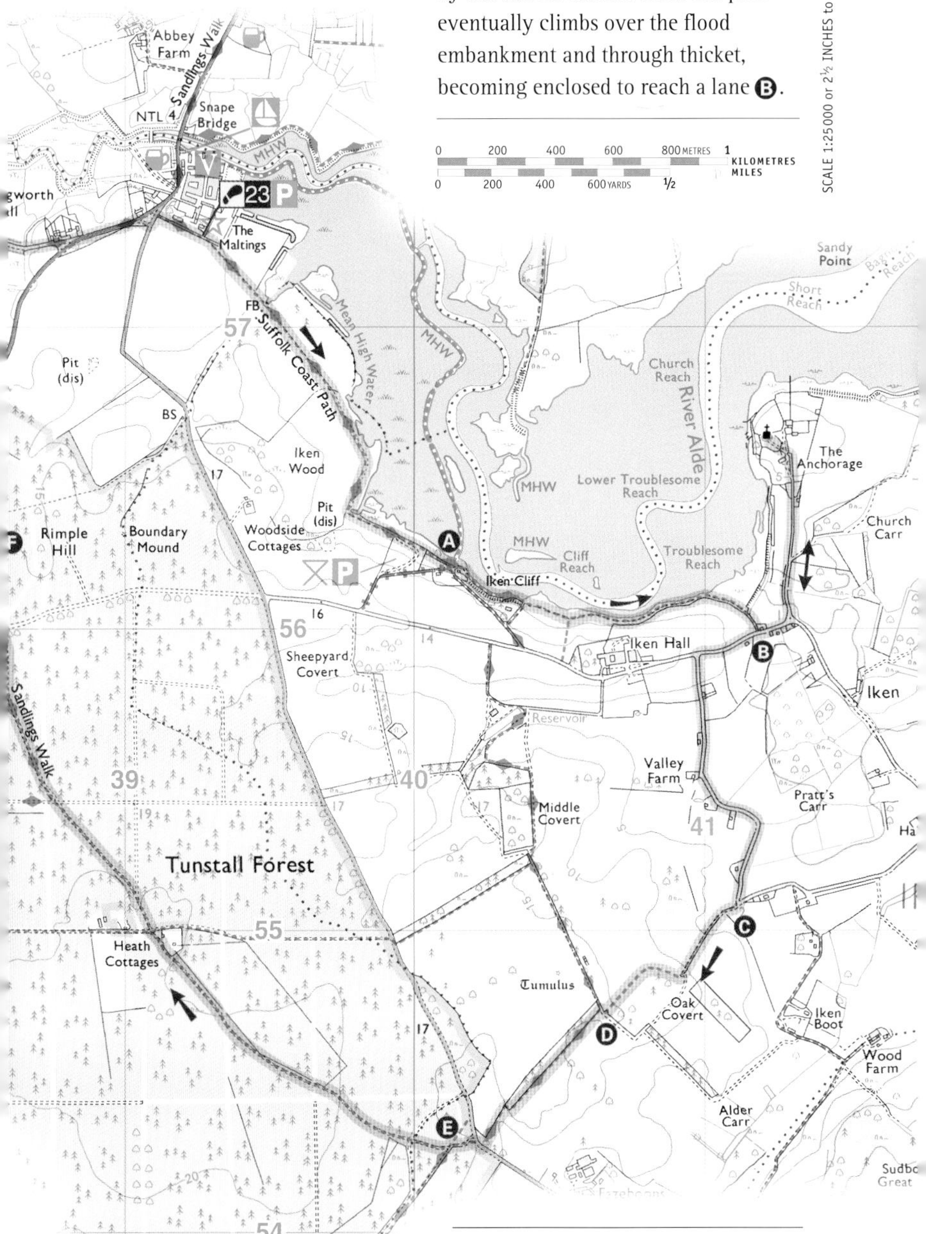

SCALE 1:25000 or 2½ INCHES to 1 MILE 4CM to 1KM

0 200 400 600 800 METRES 1
KILOMETRES
MILES
0 200 400 600 YARDS ½

Along the shore of the River Alde

Go left and then left again at a junction, following the lane to St Botolph's Church at its end. Often visited by pilgrims, it is a wonderful place for quiet reflection and, unlike many remote churches, is always open. It dates from 1450 and has a splendid font that escaped damage from bigots in the 16th and 17th centuries.

Return along the lane, continuing beyond **B** to then turn left down Sandy Lane. Follow it past several pretty cottages for ½ mile to a sharp left bend **C**. Leave there, turning right along a track marked as a footpath, and then bear left to join a sandy path along the left-hand field edge. Reaching the corner of a pinewood, bear right to follow the perimeter, passing through a gap at the far end to meet a farm track **D**.

Keep ahead for another ⅓ mile, emerging through a belt of trees onto a lane. Cross to a footpath opposite into Tunstall Forest. After a few steps turn right and then left, at a Suffolk Coast

Path waymark before reaching a fork **E**. Bear right here, leaving the Coast Path and after crossing a track the path broadens, running boldly ahead through the forest and cutting over three other tracks before reaching a junction at Heath Cottages.

Keep ahead, passing beside a barrier and shortly arriving at a fork. Bear left leaving the main track, and walking forward again at a crossing of tracks and subsequently, a narrow path. The way then soon reaches a lane. Cross to continue with the ongoing track over Blaxhall Heath, bearing right in a small clearing when it divides **F**.

Cross another road to the track opposite, the soft sand underfoot defying an energetic pace. The way finally ends at a junction of lanes. Turn right, later joining the main road to Snape, and look out for a public footpath sign to the right of the triangular village green. Follow this grassy path soon turning left along a gravel track back to the car park. ●

Barham, Baylham and Coddenham

Few country walks come better than this one. The Gipping valley features at the beginning, where you see a lovely watermill and perhaps kingfishers or even an otter. Then a path through woodland climbs out of the valley over fields and meadows to Coddenham, an attractive and unspoilt village. The way back is on field paths and through the park of Shrubland Hall, a spectacular Victorian mansion.

Note that the route encounters the busy A14 and, although there is a central refuge, care is required in crossing.

walk 24

Start
Gipping Valley Centre, Barham Picnic Site

Distance
8 miles (12.9km)

Height gain
230 feet (70m)

Approximate time
3½ hours

Route terrain
Field paths, parkland and woodland tracks

Parking
Car park at start

OS maps
Landrangers 155 (Bury St Edmunds) and 156 (Saxmundham), Explorer 211 (Bury St Edmunds & Stowmarket)

GPS waypoints
✎ TM 123 512
Ⓐ TM 121 509
Ⓑ TM 112 526
Ⓒ TM 130 542
Ⓓ TM 141 532
Ⓔ TM 143 527
Ⓕ TM 131 526
Ⓖ TM 127 523

✎ Leave by the Gipping Valley Information Centre and toilets, following a sign to the River Path past the picnic and play areas. Cross the road, descending to a path and walking left below the embankment. Turn right through a gap onto a track by a lake, unromantically called Barham B Pit, and then go left at the end on a causeway to join the riverbank by a railway bridge Ⓐ.

Head upstream to come out onto a track at Great Blakenham Lock. Cross the bridge and then take the first turning on the right. At the end, go right again along a narrow passageway between houses to regain the river. The path continues beside the water, later passing back beneath the railway. There follows a particularly beautiful section, with willows and reeds lining the bank and plenty of waterbirds and dragonflies to be seen. Upon reaching Sharn Ford Lock, there is a glimpse of Shrubland Hall and its delicate tower. The lock is one of 16 that were built in 1793 to enable barges to reach Stowmarket, 17 miles upstream from Ipswich. But with the advent of the railways, traffic declined and by the 1920s it had become disused, with the lock gates being replaced by weirs to maintain water levels in the reaches.

Passing a small car park and bridge leading to fishing pools, the way meanders on over a stile. Later mount another stile to stay beside the water, which winds past the Baylham Rare Breeds Farm (**café** open mid February to end of October) where exotic sheep and goats graze on the other side of the river. Cross a bridged ditch and then, farther on, a stream, the path soon ending at a lane beside a mill Ⓑ. Note the pretty carved heads on either side of its doorway lintel. The mill was one of 12 along the navigable stretch of the Gipping and the millwrights strongly opposed the building of the locks in order to protect their water supply. It is therefore ironic that a lock was built beside the mill, this one still with the remains of the original gate. The place has been a river crossing since at least Roman times and was controlled by a small fort on the eastern bank, Combretovium.

Over the bridge, keep ahead past the entrance to the Rare Breeds Farm to follow the Gipping Valley Circular Path along Mill Lane, disused since it was severed by the construction of the main road. Steps lead down to the busy A14 and, as traffic moves quickly, wait for a long gap in the flow before crossing each carriageway. Climb the embankment on the other side and continue over the old Norwich Road to a pleasant woodland track opposite. After a crossways overlooked by a tower the track climbs more steeply before breaking out from the trees.

Keep ahead on a hedged track and later, over a junction, Coddenham coming into view as the way then falls. When the track meets a road, cross to a path opposite that follows a hedge to a footbridge and carries on down the side of another field. Over a stile **C**, turn right, crossing a meadow to the drive from Coddenham House, which to the right, leads to a road.

The village and pub lie to the left, but the ongoing route enters the churchyard. The church is notable for its fine double hammerbeam roof embellished with angels looking down upon the nave, which is entered by a porch, oddly skewed to face the village. Leave through a kissing-gate in the south east corner. Walk on at the edge of a paddock to another kissing-gate at the foot of Broom Hill, land bought by the village in 1988. Follow a path at the lower edge of the wood, passing south-facing seats beneath oak trees that make a good place to rest. The path eventually joins a drive from a house to reach a road.

Cross to a path opposite, worn hollow by many generations of travellers who once toiled uphill by the side of pack animals, and climb a stile at the top. Pause to look back at Hemingstone Hall, a beautiful Jacobean house built of red brick, but largely hidden by trees in summer. Continue on a broad grassy track towards a farm in the middle distance.

Where the track ends, go left beside a ditch as far as a plank bridge **D**, from which a field edge path leads out to Bull's Road.

Turn right and after 200 yds take a signed footpath off on the right **E**. Cross a narrow field to the end of a

SCALE 1:25000 or 2½ INCHES to 1 MILE 4CM to 1KM

0   200   400   600   800 METRES   1
                                        KILOMETRES
                                        MILES
0   200   400   600 YARDS   ½

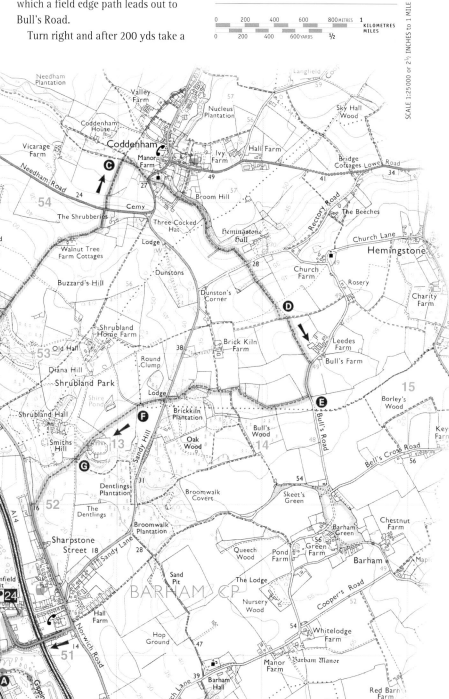

hedge, continuing with it to the corner of a wood. Over a ditch, carry on within the fringe of the trees, leaving to follow a ditch on your right. Skirt another coppice and wind on at the field edge, passing a redundant stile into the next field. Through a gap at the far side, keep going to the far-right corner, passing through thicket to a stile. Keep ahead at the edge of another wood to a stile by a pink bungalow and turn left along its driveway. Keep right as another track joins to emerge onto a lane opposite an entrance to Shrubland Park.

Follow the drive from the lodge for 200 yds to a bend, there leaving over a stile on the left **F**. Strike a right diagonal across the park to the far boundary, turning right beside it past a redundant stile to meet a drive by the stables. Shrubland Hall lies over to the right and was originally built in the Classical style by James Paine in 1770. Seventy years later Sir Charles Barry transformed it into the extravagant Italianate mansion we see today. Until recently it was the home of the Lord de Saumarez and run as a health clinic, but the settlement of death duties forced its sale in 2006.

Walk on along a path that drops below the stables to a remarkably ornate timber lodge **G**. Over a cattle-grid, leave at a footpath sign, bearing right across the park. Keep to the right of a deep pit, passing below ornamental iron gates. Picking up more fingerposts, skirt left around the far side of the pit and then bear right, a developing path taking you through trees out of the park onto a road. Go left to pass **The Sorrel Horse Inn** before turning right to cross a bridge over the A14 and return to the Gipping Valley Centre. ●

Coddenham church

Fisherman's hut, Aldeburgh

walk 25

Kersey and Hadleigh

Start
The ford, Kersey

Distance
8¼ miles (13.2km)

Height gain
410 feet (125m)

Approximate time
4 hours

Route terrain
Country lanes, field-edge and riverside paths

Parking
In The Street, Kersey

OS maps
Landranger 155 (Bury St Edmunds), Explorer 196 (Sudbury, Hadleigh & Dedham Vale)

GPS waypoints
- ✏ TM 000 441
- Ⓐ TL 982 443
- Ⓑ TL 985 432
- Ⓒ TL 992 428
- Ⓓ TM 001 426
- Ⓔ TM 003 430
- Ⓕ TM 015 418
- Ⓖ TM 025 421
- Ⓗ TM 017 424

This walk starts from one of Suffolk's prettiest villages and follows a well-waymarked route to the lovely town of Hadleigh. There is also the option of a shorter circular route around Kersey.

Kersey is one of the most popular villages in Suffolk and it is easy to see why it's so often portrayed in photographs and paintings. A haphazard collection of ancient half-timbered and thatched cottages line the main street which has a church at one end and a ford at the other.

🐾 From the ford head up past **The Bell** on your left to a bend at the top in front of the old village pump. Leave there and keep ahead along an attractive footpath, turning left at its end onto a lane. It leads past the private grounds of Priory Farm, where there are remnants of the large church that once served an Augustinian monastery founded in the 13th century. Walk along the peaceful lane for a mile to reach Seagers Cottage Ⓐ.

Immediately after, a footpath on the left crosses a plank bridge over a stream. The brook watered the moat of Lindsey Castle, a stronghold that straddled it just upstream to the right, but whose extensive earthworks are now hidden within the trees and undergrowth. Built by the Normans, the castle was still in use in c1150 at the end of their era.

The ongoing footpath strikes southwards across the middle of a field. Head towards the right hedge corner where there is a waymarker, then go across another arable field eventually emerging onto a narrow lane coming from Bridges Farm Ⓑ.

Follow it right into the hamlet of Kersey Tye, there following signs left and left again towards Kersey. Keep left at the next junction and then go along the Polstead road on the right by an attractive thatched cottage. Walk to a right-hand bend by Hart's Farm and take the track off on the left Ⓒ.

After ¼ mile the pleasant green way opens onto a field. Follow a grass path to the left, keeping ahead past the corner to drop across the field to a hedged ditch at a waymarked post Ⓓ.

The ford in the village of Kersey

Turn left beside the hedge and just before the end of the field turn right to cross a footbridge and go up a set of steps into a field. Turn left along its grassy edge past a house, to a three-way footpath signpost **E**.

If you are returning to Kersey, bear left here, cross a footbridge to a track beside Vale Cottage, turn right and keep ahead between fields, bearing left at the top to pass houses. Go forward at two successive junctions towards Kersey Street to return to the ford.

To continue to Hadleigh, turn right and head uphill along the grassy path, to the road. Bear left for a few paces and cross the road to join Coram Street. Turn right at a public footpath sign and continue beside the hedge on the right. Go through a hedge gap and keep ahead, this time with the hedge on your left. At a crossing of tracks, keep ahead in the direction of Toppesfield Bridge. At the next public footpath signpost, at a hedge gap, turn left **F**.

The path gradually descends passing to the right of Park Farm to join a long concrete track. Where this ends, turn left over the ancient packhorse bridge, Toppesfield Bridge, to visit Hadleigh. The town is well worth exploring for its wealth of medieval buildings, many of which are grouped around St Mary's Church. These include the 15th century guildhall, which was once a school, and the Deanery Tower, the remains of Archdeacon Pykenham's palace built in 1495.

The walk continues by turning left just before the bridge **G** along a path that runs beside the River Brett. This peaceful stretch of the river played an important part in Hadleigh's history as it provided power and water for the cloth trade.

After 200 yds turn left by a seat and climb the embankment to a field. Turn right and follow the field edge round to the left, then bear right at a Broom Hill footpath sign and take the path to the left of the nature reserve. Keep ahead, past a waymarker on the right, and the grassy path climbs to the brow of Constitution Hill. At the T-junction in front of a field fence turn left **H**.

Look out for where you turn right at a hedge gap then continue along the right edge of the next field to a crossing of paths. Turn right here and retrace your steps, crossing the road (A1071) and continuing into the valley to the three-way footpath sign at **E**.

Here, bear right and cross a footbridge to a track beside Vale Cottage,

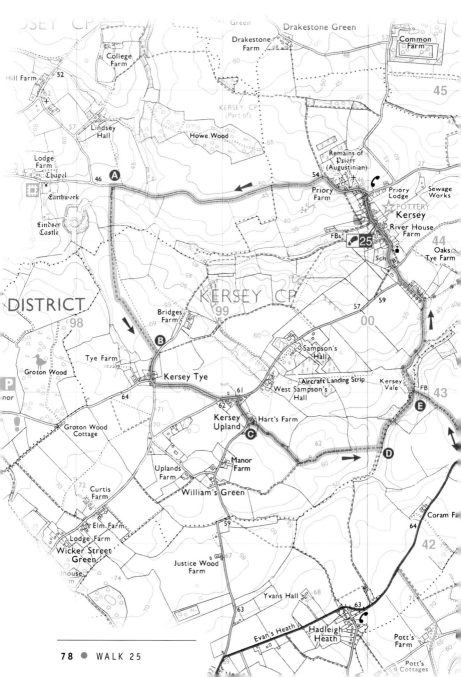

then turn right and keep ahead between fields, bearing left at the top to pass houses. Go forward at two successive junctions towards Kersey Street, the lane then dropping below the church. St Mary's has overlooked the steep valley since before the *Domesday Book*, although most of the buildings date from the 14th and 15th centuries. Inside are fragments of medieval wall painting and some fine plaster and stonework. Keep ahead along The Street to return to the ford where the walk began. ●

SCALE 1:25000 or 2½ INCHES to 1 MILE 4CM to 1KM

walk 26

Start

Thorpe Morieux

Distance

9 miles (14.4km)

Height gain

475 feet (145m)

Approximate time

4 hours

Route terrain

Quiet country lanes, field-edge paths and bridleways

Parking

Parking area just before the village hall, Bury Road

Dog friendly

On a lead through grounds to the school

OS maps

Landranger 155 (Bury St Edmunds), Explorer 211 (Bury St Edmunds & Stowmarket)

GPS waypoints

TL 942 538
Ⓐ TL 947 533
Ⓑ TL 961 536
Ⓒ TL 964 521
Ⓓ TL 964 512
Ⓔ TL 961 507
Ⓕ TL 943 505
Ⓖ TL 936 512
Ⓗ TL 936 523

Thorpe Morieux to Preston St Mary

This rural walk begins from the village of Thorpe Morieux and follows field paths and tracks, passing two churches and the peaceful village of Preston St Mary. It is a long and satisfying walk and includes a pub on the return leg.

🖉 With your back to the parking area turn right and head away from the village hall, past Sunnyside House and at the triangular green at the road junction turn right. Almost immediately, turn left along a track that passes to the right of St Mary's Church and joins a concrete track over the River Brett. Where the path ends keep head and cross a field along a grass path beside a row of telegraph poles, later bearing left to a lane Ⓐ.

Turn right along Chapel Hill and at the T-junction in front of the gates to a school, turn left towards Brettenham. At a public footpath sign in front of the village hall turn right to join a concrete track Ⓑ.

Where the track ends at Park Farm keep ahead, and after passing a pond, bear left at the waymarked post. The path soon emerges into the playing fields of Old Buckenham Hall School. Bear left along the waymarked path, which later skirts a wooded area beside an arable field. Where the path curves left just after a public footpath sign, keep ahead across the field and at the far end, cross a brick bridge at the edge of woodland. A few paces farther bear right uphill along an enclosed path to the left of woodland. Go through a wooden gate next to a house (Hitcham Lodge) and at the lane turn left. After 200 yds turn right Ⓒ along a lane.

Where the lane ends at a public footpath sign keep ahead along the left edge of a field towards trees. At the field edge turn right at a waymarker. The path curves left but before it curves again look out for where you turn right at another waymarker Ⓓ.

Head across the field bearing right in the direction of a large barn over in the distance. At the edge of the field go over a footbridge and bear left along an enclosed path beside fencing. On the right is High House Farm and its barn. Cross another footbridge and continue ahead through gates, to a track. Turn right and then right again, along a narrow lane **E**.

Just after a house turn left and go through two gates before following an enclosed path beside paddocks that descends to a gate. Keep ahead, go through another gate, cross a footbridge and follow the path, which initially runs beside a brook, before curving to go through another gate. Turn left here, initially along the left field edge then later between fields to a public footpath sign. Turn right to cross a footbridge and the path then climbs gently. At the end of the field turn right, go over another footbridge, and then turn left towards Preston Hall and the church. At the lane turn left, and enter the churchyard through a gate on the left.

Exit the churchyard into the main street via a gate and turn right past houses and just after the **Six Bells** pub, turn right at a public footpath sign

Village centre, Preston St Mary

Six Bells, Preston St Mary

beside May Cottage **F**.

The path skirts the right edge of a field before passing through a hedge gap. Turn left here, along the left field edge and cross a lane to join the path opposite. Go through a hedge gap and bear left following the field edge. The path later passes a plantation and continues along the right-hand edge of a field. Bear right through a hedge gap by a waymarker, keep ahead then follow the field as it curves left, and after 100 yds turn right to reach a lane **G**.

Turn right along the lane and as the path dips, turn left at a public footpath sign and continue along the right edge of a field. Go through a hedge gap and keep ahead towards Down Hall, turning left in front of the house by a public footpath signpost, to join a path beside the River Brett. Go through another hedge gap on the right, still following the river but looking out for where you turn right to cross a stile, to leave the riverside path.

Keep ahead, now with the hedge on your left, and maintain direction along the main path to eventually cross a concrete bridge over the river. At the end of a concrete strip turn left at a waymarker, go through a hedge gap and follow the field path left to a road **H**.

Turn right and then turn left, signposted Birds Farm. Later the track narrows and just after the farm buildings, turn right at a public footpath sign along an enclosed grassy path for about 300 yds to a path junction. Turn left here past a house and continue along the driveway to a lane. Turn right along the lane and almost immediately, turn left at a public footpath sign, and then turn right at a waymarker. Follow the field edge path to the right of a hedge to reach Bury Road where the walk began. ●

SCALE 1:25 000 or 2½ INCHES to 1 MILE 4CM to 1KM

walk 27

Start
Packhorse Bridge, Moulton

Distance
9¼ miles (14.9km)

Height gain
395 feet (120m)

Approximate time
4 hours

Route terrain
Riverside and field paths, bridleways

P Parking
Close to the bridge

Dog friendly
On a lead – many fields have livestock

OS maps
Landrangers 154 (Cambridge & Newmarket) and 155 (Bury St Edmunds), Explorer 210 (Newmarket & Haverhill)

GPS waypoints
- ✐ TL 697 645
- Ⓐ TL 712 627
- Ⓑ TL 722 621
- Ⓒ TL 726 623
- Ⓓ TL 732 633
- Ⓔ TL 741 628
- Ⓕ TL 746 637
- Ⓖ TL 719 642

Denham Castle and the three churches

Allow plenty of time for this enjoyable ramble, since there are three beautiful churches as well as the same number of pubs along the route.: The Kings Head at Moulton, Affleck Arms at Dalham, and The Chequers at Gazeley. Denham Castle, a Norman motte was built to command a wide area, and its elevated position certainly offers wonderful views across the north Suffolk countryside.

In the 15th century the River Kennett must have been a much more formidable stream than it is today and the beautiful Packhorse Bridge at Moulton would not have appeared misplaced. Today it looks stranded, as there is rarely more than a tiny stream beneath the concrete ford to lap against the piers of the bridge.

✐ Walk southwards by the trickle along Brookside, passing other bridges that take footpaths into the village. The lane finally ends beside St Peter's Church. A field track takes the way on above the river, now screened within scrub, but to the left is a typical Suffolk landscape of large fields interspersed with clumps of trees. The Icknield Way Path is claimed to follow the oldest road in Britain, running for 105 miles between Ivinghoe Beacon in Buckinghamshire and Knettishall Heath in Norfolk, and little imagination is needed to picture a packhorse train or team of oxen ambling along it.

Reaching a lane, turn right to cross Catford Bridge and then look for a footpath on the left Ⓐ into the wood. This soon leads to another field-edge path rising along the gentle valley, giving a glimpse ahead to the sail-less cap of a windmill. Eventually the path becomes contained and swings back across the tiny stream over a white bridge into Dalham. The pub lies a short way to the right, but the onward route takes you left, passing an unusual bottle-shaped brick malt kiln opposite a road climbing to the church.

Just beyond the kiln, turn right onto a footpath across the park Ⓑ that runs through an avenue of horse chestnuts up to the church. To its left and built in 1704, Dalham Hall was the childhood home of the South African Statesman, Cecil Rhodes. St Mary's Church had a spire, which fell during a great storm

The unusual malt kiln in Dalham

that swept England on the night of Oliver Cromwell's death in 1658.

Turn right to pass the church and then fork left along the drive towards Garden House, leaving left after 200 yds onto a waymarked path into the trees . There are occasional glimpses to the church and hall before the path cuts through the wood to run at its eastern edge. Waymarks guide you through the fringe of Brick Kiln Wood, crossing the edge of open ground into Blocksey Wood. Continue along the perimeter path, turning left and right at successive corners. Where the path bends left for the second time, keep ahead at a waypost, emerging over a plank bridge onto the edge of a field. Go right along the boundary, towards Desning Hall Farm. There is an outstanding view northwards towards Thetford Forest.

Walk right and wind between barns, turning right again to leave the yard. At the edge of fields, go left onto a bridleway. Although not quite the highest spot in Suffolk, the vast fields and wide sky give a rare feeling of isolation. Here, some 40 miles from the coast, the hills are nearly 350ft high, but only 10 miles or so to the north west the fenland is hardly above sea level.

Reaching the corner of a wood, keep ahead along its edge, passing through a gap into another field. Go left to the corner and into the adjacent field via a kissing-gate **E**, turning to walk with the hedge on your right. At the next corner swing left, continuing at the far side along an enclosed path that skirts the motte-and- bailey of Denham Castle. The earthwork encloses a considerable area, the castle mound rising at the northern point. The site was occupied by a Saxon lord long before the Normans arrived. However, the fortifications seen today date from the 12th century, when the country was divided by civil war after Stephen seized the throne from his cousin, Empress Matilda on the death of her father, Henry I.

Through a kissing-gate, head down the left-hand side of a field beside an orchard, dropping out at the bottom onto a lane via a kissing-gate by Castle Cottages. Turn left along the quiet byway for $^3/_4$ mile, bearing left at a Y-junction to descend a hill. Where the lane bends sharply right, look for a bridleway on the left **F**. Follow the

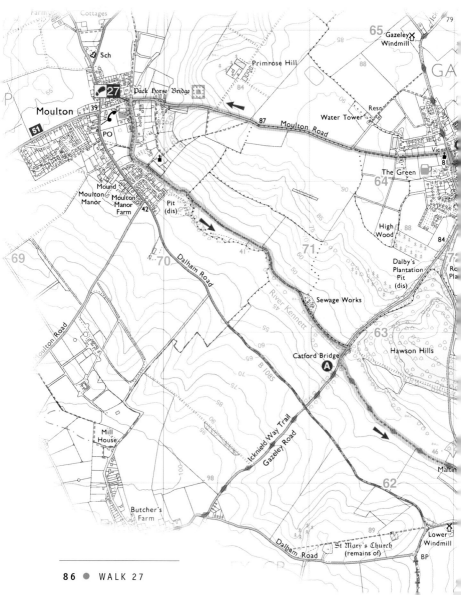

field-edge away, bearing left at a fork into the adjacent field. This is another lonely part of the walk where you are likely to have only partridges for company. The path shortly swaps to the other side of the hedge, eventually joining a tarmac track that climbs to meet a lane at Desninghall Cottages. At the telephone box go left and wind back through the farmyard, retracing your outward steps along the field edge and returning to Blocksey Wood **D**.

In the trees, turn right to rejoin the Icknield Way Path, which twists in and out of the woodland fringe as before. After crossing a footbridge, Gazeley church comes into view, the path

continuing between fields. Keep going across a final pasture to an enclosed path that emerges between houses onto the village green. Cross to an asphalt path and follow it left, keeping right at a fork onto Higham Road.

Go left to the village centre and turn right past the church, leaving along a footpath bounding the north side of the churchyard **G**. Keep forward over a drive past paddocks, eventually passing through a hedge onto Moulton Road. Ahead it leads back to Packhorse Bridge.

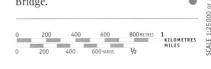

SCALE 1:25000 or 2½ INCHES to 1 MILE 4CM to 1KM

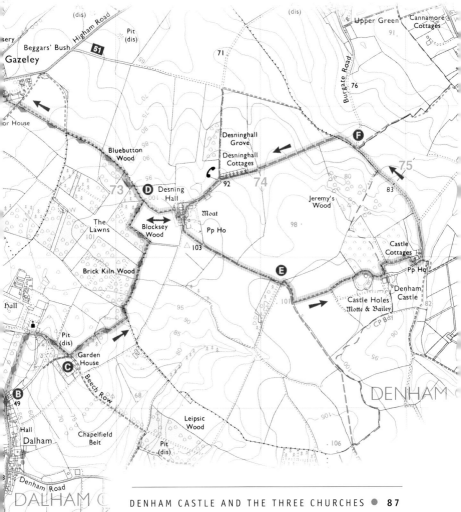

Start
Sutton Heath picnic site

Distance
10 miles (16.1km)

Height gain
295 feet (90m)

Approximate time
4½ hours

Route terrain
Sandy tracks and riverside path

Parking
At start

OS maps
Landranger 169 (Ipswich & The Naze), Explorer 197 (Ipswich, Felixstowe & Harwich)

GPS waypoints

- TM 306 475
- Ⓐ TM 320 452
- Ⓑ TM 316 449
- Ⓒ TM 307 446
- Ⓓ TM 293 450
- Ⓔ TM 283 464
- Ⓕ TM 277 485
- Ⓖ TM 297 490

Sutton Hoo, Shottisham and the River Deben

The long route begins with an enjoyable stretch over Sutton Heath on a sandy track that eventually reaches the outskirts of Shottisham. From here it strikes westwards to the River Deben, where it turns to the north, more or less following the riverbank to Methersgate Quay. After this the return route passes Sutton Hoo, where the National Trust has an interpretation centre describing one of the most important archaeological finds of English history.

From the Sutton Heath parking area, with your back to the road and the car park entrance, follow a byway heading south east. A broad, sandy track, it offers pleasant walking as it undulates gently through pine forest and at the edge of more open heath. Keep going for a little over 1½ miles to the third major junction, which is near Vale Farm. Carry on a few yards farther to leave through a gap on the right beside a waymarked post into the corner of a field Ⓐ.

Strike diagonally across towards the right-hand edge of a line of trees. Over a stile, follow a path to houses, turning right at the first cottage by a finger post. Keep ahead past an allotment and then at the edge of a field, leaving at the corner to climb a stile into a meadow. Walk on, crossing two bridged ditches in the middle. At the second of these take the waymarked path on the left Ⓑ, towards a red brick cottage near the corner of the field and climb a stile out to a lane.

Cross to a tarmac drive, marked as a bridleway, towards Wood Hall Manor. Later bear right past the entrance to the Manor, soon reaching a charming group of thatched cottages at Sutton Street Ⓒ. Fork left there, eventually reaching a junction by Pettistree Hall Farm. Turn right onto a farm track heading north, shortly meeting a crossing track near the top of the hill. Turn left along the bridleway that leads down towards the River Deben, swinging left and right as it nears the bank. When it subsequently begins to curve left again, look for a narrow waymarked path leaving on the right Ⓓ.

The path delves into the woodland bordering the riverside,

The ship burial mound at Sutton Hoo

passing The Tips, a small but scenic peninsula and popular landing spot. It later breaks out at the edge of a field before turning once more into the trees, undulating onwards to settle along a low embankment above the shore towards The Hams.

Just past Sutton Marsh Wall Sluice the bank curves left, but the path drops off right at that point to continue at the field edge. Entering woodland once more, keep left at a waymarked fork, soon emerging over a stile to run beside arable fields again. Approaching a cottage, move left onto the floodbank. The path then circles the cottage passing Methersgate Quay **Ⓔ**.

Briefly follow a track inland, and at a fence corner turn right at a public footpath sign towards the cottage. Go through a metal gate on the left and cross a paddock to leave by another gate at the far side. Keep ahead to go through two more gates, at the T-junction, bear left past a cannon at Methersgate Hall and then within a strip of pine plantation to reach a track. Go right, the drive winding past the entrance to the hall and outbuildings. Swing right and then immediately take the left grassy track, which runs away to the north at the edge of a couple of expansive fields.

Emerging through a belt of trees,

cross a track that leads to Haddon Hall, continuing beside a smaller field to another track. Again, keep ahead at the bridleway sign, and go through the gap opposite, crossing to the corner of Deben Wood. The onward way carries on at its perimeter, bending around successive corners as it gently drops into the valley.

Eventually, about 150 yds before the very bottom corner of the field, look for a gap on the right, from which steps descend through the thicket of Ferry Bank to the river **F**. The Woodbridge ferry once crossed the river from here to the town opposite, but now Wilford Bridge, $1\frac{1}{2}$ miles farther upstream, is the only option open to intending travellers.

As the ongoing path winds upriver, breaks in the trees enable views across to the boatyards. Keep going to the far end of the wood, where a fingerpost directs you off the bank. Cross a bridged ditch and walk away at the edge of a marshy meadow. Carry on as a track comes in from the right, soon joining a gravel drive. At a T-junction, go right and then bend left past a house, keeping left again past the drive to Dairy Cottage. Climb beside a wood to another junction in front of the excavation site at Sutton Hoo.

Excavations in 1939 revealed an undisturbed ship burial, thought to be that of the Anglo-Saxon warrior King Rædwald, who died c AD625. That he was a powerful man is demonstrated in the richness of the funerary goods laid beside him; a gilt and bronze helmet, elaborate broaches, a decorated shield and sword as well as a beautiful sceptre, taken to be a symbol of his rank. The finds also included silver plates, bowls, drinking horns and a massive yew vat, which it is reckoned would have held more than 22 gallons of beer. The

extensive site contains many other mounds and subsequent excavations have discovered other important treasures, for example the grave of a horse and rider.

The onward route lies to the left, shortly

passing a path off to the National Trust exhibition. Reaching a crossways beyond there, carry on ahead at the edge of vast fields on which turf for many prestigious sports pitches is grown.

Emerging onto the main road at the far side **G**, cross to Hollesley Road opposite and follow it for some 300 yds. Bear off right at a bridleway sign, heading on a shallow angle across another expanse of turf. Passing the end of a hedge, keep going with another hedgerow on your right, leaving at the far side

through a gate. A track to the right
returns you to the car park on Sutton
Heath.

SCALE 1:27777 or 2¼ INCHES to 1 MILE 3.6CM to 1KM

Further Information

 Walking Safety

Although the reasonably gentle countryside that is the subject of this book offers no real dangers to walkers at any time of the year, it is still advisable to take sensible precautions and follow certain well-tried guidelines.

Always take with you both warm and waterproof clothing and sufficient food and drink. Wear suitable footwear, such as strong walking boots or shoes that give a good grip over stony ground, on slippery slopes and in muddy conditions. Try to obtain a local weather forecast and bear it in mind before you start. Do not be afraid to abandon your proposed route and return to your starting point in the event of a sudden and unexpected deterioration in the weather.

All the walks described in this book will be safe to do, given due care and respect, even during the winter. Indeed, a crisp, fine winter day often provides perfect walking conditions, with firm ground underfoot and a clarity unique to this time of the year. The most difficult hazard likely to be encountered is mud, especially when walking along woodland and field paths, farm tracks and bridleways – the latter in particular can often get churned up by cyclists and horses. In summer, an additional difficulty may be narrow and overgrown paths, particularly along the edges of cultivated fields. Always ensure appropriate footwear is worn.

 Walkers and the Law

The Countryside and Rights of Way Act (CRoW Act 2000) extends the rights of access previously enjoyed by walkers in England and Wales. Implementation of these rights began on 19 September 2004. The Act amends existing legislation and for the first time provides access on foot to certain types of land – defined as mountain, moor, heath, down and registered common land.

Where You Can Go
Rights of Way
Prior to the introduction of the CRoW Act, walkers could only legally access the countryside along public rights of way. These are either 'footpaths' (for walkers only) or 'bridleways' (for walkers, riders on horseback and pedal cyclists). A third category called 'Byways open to all traffic' (BOATs), is used by motorised vehicles as well as those using non-mechanised transport. Mainly they are green lanes, farm and estate roads, although occasionally they will be found crossing mountainous area.

Rights of way are marked on Ordnance Survey maps. Look for the green broken lines on the Explorer maps, or the red dashed lines on Landranger maps.

The term 'right of way' means exactly what it says. It gives a right of passage over what, for the most part, is private land. Under pre-CRoW legislation walkers were required to keep to the line of the right of way and not stray onto land on either side. If you did inadvertently wander off the right of way, either because of faulty map reading or because the route was not clearly indicated on the ground, you were technically trespassing.

Local authorities have a legal obligation to ensure that rights of way are kept clear and free of obstruction, and are signposted where they leave metalled roads. The duty of local authorities to install signposts extends to the placing of signs along a path or way, but only where the authority considers it necessary to have a signpost or waymark to assist persons unfamiliar with the locality.

The New Access Rights
Access Land
As well as being able to walk on existing rights of way, under the new legislation you now have access to large areas of open land. You can of course continue to use rights of way footpaths to cross this land, but the main difference is that you can now

lawfully leave the path and wander at will, but only in areas designated as access land.

Where to Walk
Areas now covered by the new access rights – Access Land – are shown on Ordnance Survey Explorer maps by a light yellow tint surrounded by a pale orange border. New orange coloured 'i' symbols on the maps will show the location of permanent access information boards installed by the access authorities.

Restrictions
The right to walk on access land may lawfully be restricted by landowners, but whatever restrictions are put into place on access land they have no effect on existing rights of way, and you can continue to walk on them.

Dogs
Dogs can be taken on access land, but must be kept on leads of two metres or less between 1 March and 31 July, and at all times where they are near livestock. In addition landowners may impose a ban on all dogs from fields where lambing takes place for up to six weeks in any year. Dogs may be banned from moorland used for grouse shooting and breeding for up to five years.

General Obstructions
Obstructions can sometimes cause a problem on a walk and the most common of these is where the path across a field has been ploughed over. It is legal for a farmer to plough up a path provided that it is restored within two weeks. This does not always happen and you are faced with the dilemma of following the line of the path, even if this means treading on crops, or walking round the edge of the field. Although the latter course of action seems the most sensible, it does mean that you would be trespassing.

Other obstructions can vary from overhanging vegetation to wire fences across the path, locked gates or even a cattle feeder on the path.

Use common sense. If you can get round the obstruction without causing damage, do so. Otherwise only remove as much of the obstruction as is necessary to secure passage.

If the right of way is blocked and cannot be followed, there is a long-standing view that in such circumstances there is a right to deviate, but this cannot wholly be relied on. Although it is accepted in law that highways (and that includes rights of way) are for the public service, and if the usual track is impassable, it is for the general good that people should be entitled to pass into another line. However, this should not be taken as indicating a right to deviate whenever a way is impassable. If in doubt, retreat.

Report obstructions to the local authority and/or the Ramblers.

 Useful Organisations

The Broads Authority
Yare House,
62-64 Thorpe Road,
Norwich,
NR1 1RY
Tel. 01603 610734
www.broads-authority.gov.uk

Campaign to Protect Rural England
Tel. 020 7981 2800
www.cpre.org.uk

Camping and Caravanning Club
Tel. 024 7647 5426 (site bookings)
www.campingandcaravanningclub.co.uk

Forestry Commission England
East and East Midlands Area
Santon Downham
Brandon,
Suffolk
IP27 0TJ
Tel. 0300 067 4574
www.forestry.gov.uk

Long Distance Walkers' Association
www.ldwa.org.uk

Campaign for National Parks
Tel. 020 7981 0890
www.cnp.org.uk

National Trust
Membership and general enquiries:
Tel. 0344 800 1895
www.nationaltrust.org.uk
East of England Regional Office:
Tel. 01284 747500

Natural England
Norwich Regional Office
Tel. 0300 060 3900
www.gov.uk/government/organisations/
natural-england

Ordnance Survey
Tel. 03456 05 05 05
www.ordnancesurvey.co.uk

Ramblers
Tel. 020 7339 8500
www.ramblers.org.uk

Suffolk County Council
Public Rights of Way
Endeavour House,
8 Russell Road,
Ipswich IP1 2BX
Tel. 0345 606 6171
www.suffolk.gov.uk

Tourist information:
Visit East Anglia
Tel. 0333 320 4202
www.visiteastofengland.com

Local tourist information offices
(*seasonal):
Aldeburgh: 01728 453637
*Beccles: 01502 713196
Bury St Edmunds: 01284 764667
Felixstowe: 01394 383789
*Flatford: 01206 298260
Ipswich: 01473 258070
Lavenham: 01787 248207
Lowestoft: 01502 797007
Newmarket: 01638 719749
Southwold: 01502 797007
Stowmarket: 01449 676800
Sudbury: 01787 881320
Woodbridge: 01394 383599

Youth Hostels Association
Trevelyan House, Dimple Road,
Matlock, Derbyshire DE4 3YH

Tel. 01629 592700
www.yha.org.uk

 ## Ordnance Survey maps for Suffolk

The area of Suffolk is covered by Ordnance Survey 1:50 000 ($1^{1/4}$ inches to 1 mile or 2 cm to 1km) scale Landranger map sheets 134, 143, 144, 154, 155, 156, 168 and 169. These all-purpose maps are packed with information to help you explore the area. Viewpoints, picnic sites, places of interest and caravan and camping sites are shown, as well as public rights of way information such as footpaths and bridleways.

To examine the Suffolk area in more detail and especially if you are planning walks, Ordnance Survey Explorer maps at 1:25 000 ($2^{1/2}$ inches to 1 mile or 4cm to 1km) scale are ideal:

196 Sudbury, Hadleigh & Dedham Vale
197 Ipswich, Felixstowe & Harwich
210 Newmarket & Haverhill
211 Bury St Edmunds & Stowmarket
212 Woodbridge & Saxmundham
226 Ely & Newmarket
229 Thetford Forest in The Brecks
230 Diss & Harleston
231 Southwold & Bungay

The Explorer map OL40 (The Broads), at 1:25 000 scale, is also helpful.

Text:	John Brooks, Dennis and Jan Kelsall
	Revised text for 2011 edition, Deborah King
Photography:	John Brooks, Crimson Publishing, Dennis Kelsall, Deborah King
	and Peter J. Cooper, Richard Jones p.75.
	Front cover image: Shutterstock © Mel Thompson
Editorial:	Ark Creative (UK) Ltd
Design:	Ark Creative (UK) Ltd

ISBN: 978-0-31909-038-1

While every care has been taken to ensure the accuracy of the route directions, the
publishers cannot accept responsibility for errors or omissions, or for changes in details
given. The countryside is not static: hedges and fences can be removed, stiles can be
replaced by gates, field boundaries can alter, footpaths can be rerouted and changes in
ownership can result in the closure or diversion of some concessionary paths. Also,
paths that are easy and pleasant for walking in fine conditions may become slippery,
muddy and difficult in wet weather, while stepping stones across rivers and streams
may become impassable.

If you find an inaccuracy in either the text or maps, please write to Crimson
Publishing at the address below.

First published 2001 by Jarrold Publishing.
Revised and reprinted 2005 and 2007.

This edition first published in Great Britain 2011 by Crimson Publishing and reprinted
with amendments in 2017.

Crimson Publishing, 19-21C Charles Street, Bath, BA1 1HX

www.pathfinderwalks.co.uk

Printed in India by Replika Press Pvt. Ltd. 6/17

A catalogue record for this book is available from the British Library.

Front cover: Gentle evening light on the cottage at Flatford Mill
Page 1: Lavenham

Ordnance Survey

Scotland
Pathfinder Walks
3 ISLE OF SKYE
4 CAIRNGORMS
7 FORT WILLIAM & GLEN COE
19 DUMFRIES & GALLOWAY
23 LOCH LOMOND, THE TROSSACHS, & STIRLING
27 PERTHSHIRE, ANGUS & FIFE
30 INVERNESS, LOCH NESS & N-E HIGHLANDS
31 OBAN, MULL & KINTYRE
43 KYLE OF LOCHALSH
46 ABERDEEN & ROYAL DEESIDE
47 EDINBURGH, PENTLANDS & LOTHIANS

North of England
Pathfinder Walks
15 YORKSHIRE DALES
22 MORE LAKE DISTRICT
28 NORTH YORK MOORS
35 NORTHUMBERLAND & the SCOTTISH BORDERS
39 DURHAM, NORTH PENNINES & TYNE
    AND WEAR
42 CHESHIRE
49 VALE OF YORK & YORKSHIRE WOLDS
53 LANCASHIRE
60 LAKE DISTRICT
63 PEAK DISTRICT
64 SOUTH PENNINES
70 NORTH EAST ENGLAND HERITAGE WALKS
71 THE HIGH FELLS OF LAKELAND
73 MORE PEAK DISTRICT

Short Walks
1 YORKSHIRE DALES
2 PEAK DISTRICT
3 LAKE DISTRICT
13 NORTH YORK MOORS
20 CHESHIRE & THE GRITSTONE EDGE

Wales
Pathfinder Walks
10 SNOWDONIA
18 BRECON BEACONS
32 NORTH WALES AND SNOWDONIA
34 PEMBROKESHIRE & CARMARTHENSHIRE
41 MID WALES & THE MARCHES
55 GOWER, SWANSEA & CARDIFF

Short Walks
14 SNOWDONIA
25 AROUND CARDIFF
31 BRECON BEACONS

Heart of England
Pathfinder Walks
6 COTSWOLDS
14 SHROPSHIRE & STAFFORDSHIRE
20 SHERWOOD FOREST & THE EAST MIDLANDS
29 WYE VALLEY & FOREST OF DEAN
33 SHAKESPEARE COUNTRY & VALE OF EVESHAM
40 MORE COTSWOLDS

Short Walks
4 COTSWOLDS
32 HEREFORDSHIRE & THE WYE VALLEY

East of England
Pathfinder Walks
44 ESSEX
45 NORFOLK
48 SUFFOLK
50 LINCOLNSHIRE & THE WOLDS
51 CAMBRIDGESHIRE & THE FENS

Short Walks
33 NORFOLK INTO SUFFOLK

South West of England
Pathfinder Walks
1 SOUTH DEVON & DARTMOOR
5 CORNWALL
9 EXMOOR & THE QUANTOCKS
11 DORSET
21 SOMERSET, THE MENDIPS & WILTSHIRE
26 DARTMOOR
68 NORTH AND MID DEVON
69 SOUTH WEST ENGLAND COASTAL WALKS

Short Walks
8 DARTMOOR
9 CORNWALL
10 SOMERSET FROM BATH TO THE QUANTOCKS
19 DORSET
21 EXMOOR
28 WILTSHIRE FROM SALISBURY TO THE KENNET
29 SOUTH DEVON

South East of England
Pathfinder Walks
8 KENT
12 NEW FOREST, HAMPSHIRE & SOUTH DOWNS
25 THAMES VALLEY & CHILTERNS
37 LONDON'S PARKS & COUNTRYSIDE
54 HERTFORDSHIRE & BEDFORDSHIRE
65 SURREY
66 WEST SUSSEX & THE SOUTH DOWNS
67 EAST SUSSEX & THE SOUTH DOWNS
72 COUNTRY WALKS NEAR LONDON

Short Walks
7 THE CHILTERNS
23 NEW FOREST NATIONAL PARK
24 SUSSEX & SOUTH DOWNS
27 ISLE OF WIGHT

Practical Guides
GPS FOR WALKERS
MAP READING SKILLS
THE COUNTRYSIDE COMPANION